The Lakes of I

The Lakes of North Wales

by Jonah Jones

Whittet Books Ltd London

First published 1983 by Wildwood House
This edition published 1987
Text and illustrations copyright © 1983 Jonah Jones
Maps copyright © 1983 Keith Trodden

Whittet Books Ltd, 18 Anley Road, London W14 0BY

British Library Cataloguing in Publication Data

Jones, Jonah
   The lakes of North Wales.
   1. Lakes – Wales, North – Description and
   travel   2. Wales, North – Description and travel
   I. Title
   914.29′104858   DA740.N6

   ISBN 0 905483 54 5

Printed by Biddles Ltd
Bound by Camelot Press

Title page illustration: Deobadarn Castle

Contents

To David, Peter and Naomi

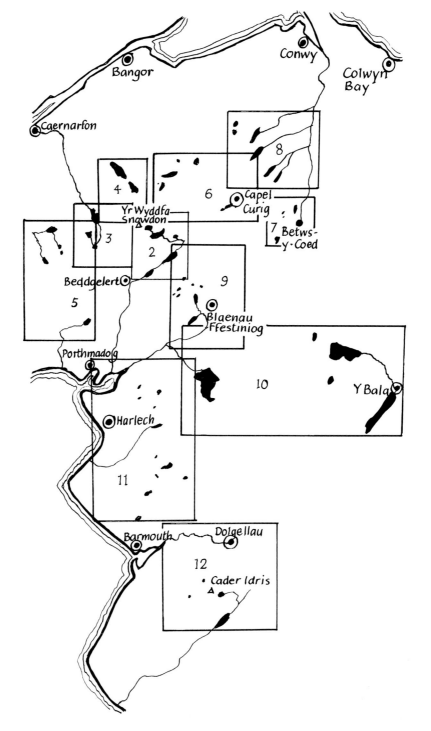

Bangor

Conwy

Colwyn
Bay

Caernarfon

8

4

6

Capel
Curig

Yr Wyddfa
Snowdon

7   Betws-
     y-Coed

3

2

9

Beddgelert

5

Blaenau
Ffestiniog

Porthmadog

10

Y Bala

Harlech

11

Barmouth   Dolgellau

12

Cader Idris

Foreword

This is a book primarily for walkers, though lakes have interest for people who may not regard walking as an activity of value in itself. I have indicated specific lakes where botanists, naturalists, historians, even engineers might find something of interest beyond the athletic challenge and aesthetic pleasure which are the laudable aims of walkers.

But there is an incidental, and I believe important, motive behind writing about the lakes of North Wales at this moment. In my own lifetime, quite a few of the lakes have been changed so drastically that this book bears the intention of recording the lakes as they stand at present.

A complex mountainous region like North Wales is not easy to divide into logical compartments for the listing of its lakes. Strictly speaking, a specific drainage system ought to solve the problem, from source to sea, taking in the lakes along the system. But while it works in some cases, in others it does not. So while some chapters are based on systems, like the Llanberis lakes, others are based on a geographical location or centre, like Capel Curig.

Naming is not as easy as it may appear. I am conscious that although Welsh is the oldest living language spoken in these islands, it can present difficulties to travellers. Even among the Welsh themselves, there are occasional inconsistencies in spelling place names, such as Arenig or Arennig. When the narrow gauge railway was built in the last century to link the quarries of Blaenau Ffestiniog with Portmadoc, it was named the Festiniog Railway, with one 'f' in the Anglicized way. Today's railway enthusiasts, correctly in my opinion, have preserved this inaccurate but historic form. Portmadoc has lately been restored to its more proper Welsh form of Porthmadog.

Over the years, the Ordnance Survey has sometimes changed. Thus, Llyn Morwynion in 1838 has become Llyn Morynion in 1974. This may seem tiresome, but Welsh is a living language with a lively oral tradition, and I am with T. E. Lawrence on this. When publishing *Seven Pillars of Wisdom*, his proof-reader asked for consistency of Arabic names. Lawrence replied: 'I spell my names anyhow, to show what rot systems are!'

I am grateful to Professor Gwyn Jones for permission to quote from both his *Prospect of Wales* (Penguin, 1948) and his translation of *The Mabinogion* (with Professor Thomas Jones, Everyman's Library, 1949).

My thanks are due also to the Photography Department staff of the National College of Art and Design in Dublin for advice and assistance with photography.

For the maps I must thank Keith Trodden.

Nor should this opportunity pass without mention of my gratitude to my son Peter, who accompanied me on many of the lake walks and made his inimitable contribution to our lay researches in geology, natural history or whatever might distinguish such and such a lake.

And, of course, my gratitude to my wife Judith Maro, who patiently deciphered and typed my manuscript.

Lastly, it must be stressed that indication of a route to a lake does not imply a Right of Way.

JONAH JONES

One   The Lakes

There is such an attraction about a sheet of water in a landscape that where men have felt its absence they have gone to great lengths to create one. The latest, in front of the University of East Anglia in Norwich, is a case in point, also 'Lake Carter' at Lancaster University with its superb water-lilies.

In the closing years of his life at Giverny, the French Impressionist Claude Monet enjoyed diverting the little streams of the Epte to create lily pools of surpassing beauty, and his paintings of them in the Jeu de Paume are meditations on time. Their quality removes them from the tensions of so much of Western art. Their spirit was more oriental than occidental in that calm we associate with Japanese painters like Hiroshige and his *hakkei* (eight views) of landscapes like Lake Biwa. The Taj Mahal's more formal stretch of water comes to mind too, and the ornamental pool that leads up to the old pin mill in the gardens of Bodnant is hardly less beautiful.

For the most part, lakes impart such peace that men will stand by them for hours. The lakes of North Wales on certain days take on this calm beauty, when only the wakes of Little Grebe disturb the glassy surface, most often of an evening. On other days, the winds can lash waves against their shaly beaches with a fury reminiscent of the sea.

Natural lakes have that advantage. They are mostly untamed, and they are almost never without interest or aesthetic delight of some kind. Often they possess an iridescent beauty, like jewels in their setting, at other times are forbidding in their black austerity.

Compared with the lakes of Cumbria which have earned the universal accolade of being called the Lake District, as though no other existed, the lakes of North Wales have never been so celebrated, and whereas the Lake District seems to have enjoyed perpetual homage for its wild beauty, the North Wales lakes have sometimes in the past evoked more a curiosity about their local lore than a reverence for their beauty.

Gwyn Jones in *A Prospect for Wales* sums it up admirably:

> There is, for example, the contrast often made between Snowdonia and the Lake District, between the haunting unease of the one and the friendly sparkle of the other, between sombre mountain and dappled fell. Yet the difference, and it is undoubted, is not to be measured in height of hill or depth of valley, in angle of rock or altitude of tarn. It is a difference of atmosphere, and may with propriety be termed spiritual. Mainly it consists in the sense of human history, unhappy human history, with which every foot of Snowdonia is richly and affectingly charged.

Llyn Edno

Is it legend or history that connects King Arthur with Llyn Teyrn, 'Lake of the Monarch'? However that may be, what is certain is that Snowdonia and its lakes was the area where hard-pressed Celtic chieftains held out for generations against increasing pressures from the east.

So, for a variety of reasons, the lakes of North Wales have enjoyed less renown for their own sake than their counterparts in Cumbria. Yet they are *there*, even describing much the same radial pattern as do the Cumbrian lakes. Their flora, fauna and environmental patterns are not dissimilar. Relative to their attendant mountain masses, however, the Welsh lakes are smaller than the Cumbrian ones, and this may explain in part their comparative want of celebrity. People will visit Cumbria for its lakes, whereas they will visit Wales for its mountains.

Then, too, of course, there is the little matter of history and tradition. In 1768, the publication of a poem by J. Dalton and a letter by a Dr Brown sent John Gray and Andrew Young haring off to the Lake District. Two years later it had become fashionable to tour 'the English lakes' and the habit has not ceased to this day.

Wales, by contrast, seemed to figure as a sort of dark continent to the Romantic sensibility of the eighteenth and nineteenth centuries. Even Eleanor Butler and Sarah Ponsonby, the celebrated Ladies of Llangollen, settled on the edge of the wilder area in the bosky valley of the Dee and seemed only to travel down in the Oswestry direction and never up towards the mountains and the lakes.

Lakes must be searched out, and many travellers in the past kept to the roads and ventured one or two peaks for the record. A.G. Bradley (1898) is typical. Passing from Capel Curig to Ogwen, an area particularly rich in lakes, he says: 'Hopeless as it would be to attempt here a notice of the numerous lakes and tarns and waterfalls that lie buried amid the mountains on either hand, I may perhaps indulge in one backward glance across the valley to the gloomy glen that comes down from one of the wildest and most sombre Welsh tarns, Llyn Idwal.' As we shall see, that would not take him much out of his way, since Idwal is less than half an hour by an easy track from Telford's road, the present A5 linking London and Holyhead.

Although the Romantic Joseph Cradock (1770) introduced the idea that 'Wild Wales' might be viewed for its scenery, his prose is high-flown and extreme, given to encounters with 'poor, blind harpers' and native country girls ready at the drop of a hat, or a penny, to break into music and dancing for the delectation of travellers. He was much too busy collecting these fables from doubtful sources to give much attention to lakes such as the beautiful Llyn Cwellyn (he called it 'Cychwhechlyn', making a thorough meal of his Welsh), which lay along his route.

H.P. Wyndham in 1774 already noticed this comparative neglect of Wales. As he says in his Introduction to *A Tour through Wales and Monmouthshire* (1781):

> Notwithstanding this, the Welsh tour has been hitherto strangely neglected; for while the English roads are crowded with travelling parties of pleasure, the Welsh are so rarely visited that the author did not meet with a single party during his six weeks' journey through Wales.
>
> We must account for this from the general prejudice which prevails, that the Welsh roads are impracticable, the inns intolerable, and the people insolent and brutish.
>
> The writer of these sheets is happy that he is enabled to remove such discouraging difficulties, and assures the reader that in the low, level counties, the turnpikes are excellent; that the mountain roads are, in most parts, as good as the nature of the country will admit of; that the inns, with the exception of a few, are comfortable; and that the people are universally civil and obliging.

Perhaps it was the language, the English never having understood the Welshman's attachment to it. Would it not have been more convenient to Romantic travellers if the natives had dropped this tiresome impediment to social intercourse? George Borrow, to be fair, mastered the language before travelling in Wales and enjoyed 'breaking the code' on occasion, to the great discomfiture of the calumniating postman at Betws Garmon:

Suddenly he began speaking Welsh to the people; before, however, he had uttered two sentences the woman lifted her hand with an alarmed air, crying 'Hush! he understands.' The fellow was turning me to ridicule. . . . The fellow stood aghast; his hand trembled, and he spilt the greater part of the whisky on the ground. . . . Then going up to the man I put my right forefinger very near to his nose, and said 'Dwy o iaith dwy o wyneb, two languages two faces, friend!'

So perhaps there are reasons for the comparative want of celebrity. Unaccountable, though, is the indifference to the beauty of many smaller lakes in North Wales, whereas a number of Cumbrian ones, often under the old Norse name of tarn, are celebrated for their own sake.

It may be also, as with Ireland (most Irish people in Ireland now regard the good Irish name 'Eire' as condescending from the mouth of an Englishman), that there are inherent difficulties of nomenclature, depending on where you are and 'whose side you are on'.

Unlike the 'Lake District', which is comparatively compact and self-entire, the mountains (and therefore the lakes) of North Wales are difficult to delineate. 'North Wales', for a start, stretches east as far as Wrexham, or for some people merely means that stretch of seaside resorts from Llandudno to Prestatyn.

'Snowdonia' is an ugly *ersatz* word which I personally dislike, but which fits our present purpose well enough and has by now really entered the language as 'Snowdonia National Park'. But it is stretching a point, for neither Cader Idris nor Ardudwy *feels* like 'Snowdonia' to me.

Snowdonia, roughly speaking, might be more properly taken as that mountainous region dominated by the peak and outliers of Yr Wyddfa (the Welsh name for the actual peak of Snowdon). But this would exclude, strictly speaking, several exciting tracts of mountainous country. The old words Caernarvonshire and Merioneth would have suited our purpose best, but are now disappearing from the language, alas. So stretching the point, as with 'Snowdonia National Park', seems the only answer in the end.

Icing on Llyn Llydaw

Even the most recent realignment of counties has got this area wrong. (It is not unique there, and most English counties have been decimated to give way to meaningless administrative districts.) Gwynedd to the Welsh has always denoted the mountainous fastness which was once an easily identifiable kingdom of the mountains round Eryri, and the name has now been exploited to cover an even greater area outside that traditional tract.

Since the lakes east of the Vale of Conwy are mostly reservoirs, either man-made or extended, and the heavily glaciated mountainous area of natural lakes really lies west of the Afon Conwy, it is safe enough to use the name 'Snowdonia' for the purpose of this book.

West of the Conwy, north of and including Cader Idris, fairly covers the area of mountains of North Wales while being quite (but not clearly) distinct from mid-Wales. Thus Llyn Vyrnwy and Llyn Clywedog are excluded, since they lie well outside the line of the Bala-Talyllyn fault, which is the one distinct break in any progress from North to mid-Wales. But mountainous terrain does not cease from North to South Wales, so nowhere are the divisions as distinct as with the Lake District, where you pretty well know when you are *out* of it.

So all told, even its identity has militated against North Wales as a discrete area of lakes compared with its more compact rival. And yet the lakes of North Wales are beautiful by any standard – and the twin lakes of Llynnau Gwynant and Dinas under Yr Wyddfa's southern flank must be among the best in their setting in Britain and are visited by a host of travellers.

For my part, I have gradually trimmed my walking activities over the years and the lakes have attracted my attention increasingly, not as features on the way to some height, but as destinations in themselves. The variety of their environments, of their shapes, colours, moods, and in some cases of their legends, is always diverting. Still enjoying the physical stress of tackling the slopes, I confess that my personal liking is for some of the more deserted lakes up on the flanks of the mountains. Some are hardly visited and access to them is difficult enough for them to remain so. In particular, many are best seen in winter, when the ubiquitous green of the fescue grass and bracken gives way to shades of ochre and copper.

Yes, the lakes are there, in varying degrees of splendour and isolation for our private delectation. But how did they come to be there? To answer that question is often to enhance one's appreciation.

In the Primary Era of geological time the underlying pre-Cambrian and Cambrian rock strata of Snowdonia suffered such cataclysmic terrestrial stress that they buckled in a roughly south-west to north-east bias, the 'Caledonian Trend'. At the same time, a great amount of submarine volcanic activity (for North Wales was then under the sea, as many a fossil evidences, even as high as Yr Wyddfa) left the igneous masses that shape so many of the mountains we know today. The best example is slightly to the west of the lake area, in Yr Eifl group, where Trefor granite has been quarried for centuries. Its toughness has even supplied material for those sculpturesque curling stones that Scotsmen glide and guide with besoms over the ice.

When this great mass then rose out of the sea in the next earth movement, it was one extensive rippling dome stretching from Cader Idris in the south to Yr Wyddfa in the north.

But the major actual determinant in the formation of the lakes was glaciation, the last of the factors in geological time. The valleys which hold the lakes were scooped out by the glaciers of the Ice Age. Roughly speaking, this began one million years ago and ended only some ten thousand years ago, a period marked by the emergence of man, though almost certainly not in the then inhospitable wastes of North Wales. A complex of glaciers flowed in roughly the same direction as the valleys we know now, following mostly the slight rain-water channels that preceded them. For at first the upraised massif was cut only by rain-water, and the glaciers tended to follow and deepen their trail, though in one valley at least, now occupied by Llyn Tegid (Bala) and Llyn Mwyngil (Talyllyn) the host valley was more pronounced, in fact a rift valley. It needed only the glaciers' melt and subsequent rainfall to fill the scooped out hollows with water.

The climate of North Wales is distinctive. Living where I do on Traeth Bach, south of the mountains, you can watch the weather approaching. It rolls in fresh from the Atlantic up the St George's Channel, imparting quite different conditions from those pertaining in much of England, where many a winter month can be locked in a dank earth-bound mist. The greatest contributor to the lakes is of course the rainfall. Up at Llyn Glaslyn as much as 188 inches of rain was recorded in 1946 and even a drought year will register more than 100 inches. There are days when the streams and waterfalls feeding the lakes turn white with anger as they carry the water off the rock slopes. The best time to follow a stream up to a lake is often just as the rain is clearing, when the clouds lift majestically off the peaks like fingers after a too demonstrative caress and the sun breaks through a sky awash with the purest light.

In winter, some upper lakes freeze. The coastal belt of North Wales enjoys comparatively mild winters, but on the heights you can watch the brittle ice patterns actually forming after a night of frost. There is such silence that a raven's harsh cry echoes from the frozen crags of the corrie with crystal clarity.

Traeth Bach

Then in summer, when a hand dipped in a lake registers a deep chill, thunder clouds can gather in the corries and blacken the waters. The riffling winds circle wickedly over the lakes and send a black shiver like shot silk over their surface. Sometimes, as in Cwm Idwal, a wind seems to have its origin there, for no apparent reason, and in no time is carrying eddying funnels of spray off the lake a hundred feet up into the air, as though in answer to some mere mortal challenge. Sailors down in the Menai Straits would have it so, once upon a time, when Idwal was a dark and remote fastness visited only by the mad and the bad.

No lake is the same two days running, and the difference between the seasons is much more extreme than a summer visitor might believe.

The lakes themselves vary enormously, from a high rock-bound cirque lake like Llyn Dulyn with its small area and great depth, to tree-girt Llyn Tegid nearly four miles long in its rift valley, with the sailing dinghies skimming over its waves.

It is nearly always possible to attach a meaning to the names of Welsh lakes, even if at times it may seem obscure, as in the case of Llyn Cwm-Ystradllyn, literally 'Lake of the Valley of the Lake's Strand [shore]', which could apply to so many of the lakes. Many of the names suggest great beauty; for instance, Ffynnon Lloer, 'Well of the Moon', where tradition enhances that beauty, for it is said that the moon must be seen in it once a month, a memory of an old superstition. Marchlyn Mawr (alas, now part of the new pump storage scheme at Llanberis) means the 'Great Horse Lake', possibly because of a nearby plot of land called Rhos Marchlyn, on which colts were turned out for the summer. Llyn Teyrn, 'Lake of the Monarch', may commemorate King Arthur, whose exploits and death are remembered at various locations on Yr Wyddfa. There are two Llynnau Morwynion, 'Lakes of the Maidens', one of which recalls a sad fable from *The Mabinogion*.

Sometimes the names express a sadness that reflects the lake's aspect. Llyn Idwal is a case in point, the big lateral moraine at its side being the legendary grave of the Giant Idwal.

In other cases a more homely connotation sets the mind wandering. Why Llyn Ffynnon-y-Gwas, 'Lake of the Man-Servant's Well', I wonder? Was it his very own, high up on Yr Wyddfa's western flank, where no master's shout could disturb his extra-terrestrial meditations? Poor little Llyn-y-Biswail – however did it come to earn its humble name 'Lake of Dung'? Its location high on the watershed between Cwm Croesor and Cwmorthin could hardly have been the local midden.

Two lakes commemorate early Celtic saints, Padarn and Peris, while one commemorates a mere maid, Elsi, who must have been some girl to deserve such beauty for herself. Occasionally topography dictates a name, as in Llyn Cwm-Corsiog, 'Lake of the Marshy Hollow' or Llynnau Diffwys, 'Lakes of the Precipice'.

But inevitably, even in Welsh, a few names are shrouded in mystery. 'Lake of the Bubbling Water' has been suggested for Llyn Llagi under the brow of Cnicht, and though I would not take away any of its beauty, it is no more appropriate for Llyn Llagi than for many another. Though there is no Welsh word *llugwy*, the broad sense of 'Well of Clear Water' for Ffynnon Llugwy is surely right. But I know of no meaning for Llyn Stwlan, once an obscure corrie lake between the two Moelwyns, and now the upper point of the Tan-y-Grisiau Pump Storage Scheme.

It is interesting to speculate on the appearance of the lakes as they formed after the melting of the glaciers. For lakes are anything but immutable. As soon as they were made they began to silt up, and the streams flowing out of them gradually cut a deeper floor in the barrier of rock or moraine that held them back and thus in time lowered the level of the lake. Some lakes have disappeared altogether, leaving flat green meadow-land as in Nant Ffrancon or around Beddgelert. Others have been divided by lateral deltas, like Llynnau Peris and Padarn. The flora and fauna of the lakes and their environment have changed over the centuries as levels, deposits, weather and the mark of man have changed. Native deciduous forest, mostly the hardy sessile oak, once clothed the shapes of the surrounding hills, and in a few places only does it persist, as at Llyn Padarn. Around the lakes and their associated swampy areas, alder would predominate. Domestic animals hardly existed. Rabbits, beaver and deer were more common. The beaver was prevalent up to the tenth century and its mark on the rivers and lakes must have been considerable. Except that the forest was deciduous and not coniferous, the aspect of some of the valley lakes must have resembled present-day Canadian lakes. Certainly beaver was not only present but came to represent a sort of currency, for the laws of Hywel Dda in the tenth century decreed that a beaver pelt be valued at sixpence, fifteen times that of an ox, and this may be one of the earliest legislative measures to affect the ecology. It is surely one of the earliest examples of a native species that became extinct in the country. Deer roamed the woods round the lakes till 1626.

Then as agrarian civilization advanced up the valleys, there was much wood-clearing and extending of hay-meadows. Near Llyn Eigiau, for instance, four substantial houses were built in 1554, maintaining 100 cattle.

Overleaf Llyn Padarn

But, excepting the decimation of native forests in the valleys and slopes, many of the lakes, especially the higher ones, have changed little in the last half millennium. Lateral boundary *ffridd* walls built in the eighteenth and nineteenth centuries across the lower mountain slopes still stand the test of time and weather. They kept the cattle to the valley bottoms and the sheep to the upper slopes except in winter. About this period, too, many of the slopes above the lakes were mined for metal ores and spoil-heaps still scar the scree and heather.

The mines are no longer worked, but nature has a tender way of clothing the crumbling walls of the buildings with lichen and even foliage, and the spoil heaps with stonecrop and a variety of persistent mosses and grasses. However, the lakes are still endangered by man. If there seems nothing we can do to save some of them from development in schemes like pump-storage reservoirs, at least we can all do something to prevent the spread of litter along their shores. Over the last decade, even the highest lakes have not been free from beer and Coca-Cola tins. I find it difficult to understand why walkers who make the effort to climb to some lake, presumably to enjoy the environment and the view, then fling their discards in its prize adornment.

By now designation of the National Park stresses care for the environment. Wardens are among a host of people dedicated to the care of the lakes in their setting. But odd things happen inadvertently, even with the best intentions in the world. At one stage in the '50s and early '60s, agricultural pesticides were beginning to decimate certain bird species, in particular herons, but at present this trend seems to be abating and I have seen herons at quite high altitudes by the side of a lake. The swan population on Traeth Mawr has increased dramatically over the last few years and I hope 'the territorial imperative' will guide them to some of the lakes higher up the Glaslyn system. Recently I noted that a pair with three cygnets had settled on Llyn Mair near Maent-wrog.

The lakes have meant different things to different people, and the aesthetic pleasure which is the chief motivation of this book is probably the most recent response. Travellers in the past, like Samuel Johnson, could sometimes pass a lake with complete indifference, and even the most graphic of travellers, George

Borrow, when he did notice a lake, usually noted only two
things, its depth and the size of its fish. Curious legends about the
lakes seem to have interested early travellers, from Giraldus
Cambrensis (1188) to Thomas Pennant (1784), and sometimes a
story by an earlier traveller has provided the motive for a visit to a
lake by a later one, as for instance the tale of 'the floating island' in
Llyn-y-Dywarchen.

Of course, the lakes have always been of interest to anglers, and
some of them, like Llyn Dwythwch, have appeared in Memorial
Rolls as sources of wealth for their fishing. I do not fish, but I
confess to sometimes envying anglers for the obvious pleasure
they derive from the lake, for they stand there in utter peace (at
least I suppose it is peace – who knows what bloody turmoil goes
on in those inscrutable minds?) working out ways of snaring their
subaqueous quarry, often invoking other magical forms of nature
in the way of flies like 'Partridge's and Hare's ear' or 'Jay wing
with black body and ginger hackle'. Anglers often jealously guard
their lakes against intruders and can be relied upon to preserve
them in pristine glory.

That old classic *Mountains of Snowdonia* has a most diverting chapter, 'Notes on Angling', full of esoteric advice mysterious to the mere layman

> Llyn Cwm Ffynnon – swarms with hungry trout six to the pound. Sometimes get three at once. Good fighters. Waders useful. Best by island and off reeds. Boat broken . . . Llyn Elsi – Reservoir, drinking supply and electric light for Bettws-y-Coed . . . fish up to 5¼ lbs taken, average about 16 oz. Teal and greenfly deadly, July and August in evening. Worming allowed.

Then, this piece of homely advice: 'The man who sells the licence is usually a keen angler who will give good response to a friendly and diplomatic approach.'

The more I read such things and see anglers calmly about their chosen vocation, the more I am tempted to take up their very contemplative pursuit.

Water lilies on Llyn Mair

But on the fish no two anglers seem to agree, which only goes to confirm the general opinion that they are less than truthful about the fish they land. The *torgoch* (Welsh char, or 'red belly') is a legendary fish in North Wales which really exists and has been recorded by travellers throughout the centuries (sometimes, I suspect, without their having ever actually seen the specimen), but whether in one lake now, or in four or more, is hard to establish. Bruce Campbell is of the opinion that this 'may be due to their inability to compete with an artificial increase in the number of trout in the same lake'.

For naturalists lakes carry enormous interest. If compared with Cumbria, North Wales took much longer to attract the general traveller, naturalists were early on the scene and despite the much more arduous terrain before the development of roads, nothing seemed to deter them. Dr J. J. Dillenius in 1726, with Samuel Brewer, climbed the Glyders and explored Llyn-y-Cwn to examine its flora, finding pill-wort, quillwort and shoreweed. Now by any standards, even today, that represents quite a day's work, since the Glyders are well over 3,000 feet, Llyn-y-Cwn well over 2,500 feet above sea level – and the going is as rough as it comes. But the next day the intrepid pair were around Llanberis cataloguing gentian, Welsh poppy and water lobelia.

Though Daniel Defoe in his *Tour of England and Wales* seems like most travellers to have avoided the mountains like a plague, he did most conscientiously mention the *torgoch* by its Welsh name at Llanberis.

The greatest traveller/naturalist of all was Thomas Pennant, of course, and his classic *A Tour of Wales* (1784) remains a point of reference still. Many of the ascents and rock-climbs in the area were first pioneered by naturalists, in particular botanists, who would go to any lengths to get a rare specimen from an inaccessible ledge. The French botanist, J. Gay, listed every lake in Eryri and recorded 'echantillons' of quillwort from the vast majority, though the rare *I. Echinospora* occurred only in the Llanberis lakes. That was in 1862.

The dominant flora in and around the lakes of North Wales are recorded best by Condry, and most especially, from my own observation, the lake bottom flora: shoreweed, awlwort, water lobelia, common quillwort and small quillwort, and of course the white and yellow water-lilies.

The flora differ greatly, depending on the base minerals draining into the lake with the rainfall. Llyn Idwal, because of its base-rich catchment area, is among the richest, a quite dense floor-covering, looking in certain lights from above like a lush carpet. In quieter lakes, like Llyn Mwyngil (Talyllyn), the water-lily flourishes, and is a special hybrid in that lake.

Reeds are not very frequent, the waters being mostly too turbulent from the fairly constant winds in the area. In one case at least, Llyn Tegid, their presence has been affected by the interference of man altering the depth of the lake.

The most beautiful example of the effect of reeds breaking the surface of a lake is the head of Llyn Crafnant, where their verticality in the horizontal waters can be most striking against the evening sun before it dips over the crags at the head of the valley. In some lakes flotegrass adds a decorative element to the surface.

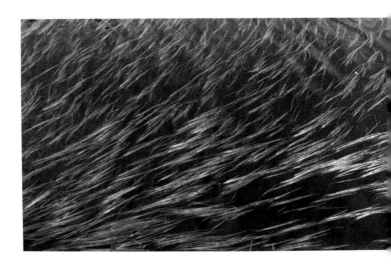

Flote grass

28

Sphagnum moss: Llyn Tecwyn Isaf

At the edge of the lakes, the first evidence of alluvial silting is the extent of peat and sphagnum moss, out of which rise shrubs like the fragrant bog myrtle and even trees like birch, as at Llyn Tecwyn Isaf. On the drier slopes above lakes, there is often an abundance of that beautiful little quatrefoil flower *Potentilla tormentil*, pale yellow stars in a green firmament; and closer in, where bog conditions prevail, the bog asphodel provides a foil for the spotted orchid.

In all, the lakes and their borders are rich in flora which, if not as rare and precious as some of the hardy alpine species that persist in crannies in some of the north-facing cwms, make up in sheer beauty of form and colour out of an abundance of moisture.

I have seen the edge of a lake white with bog cotton, but even whiter are those silted-up hollows which once held a lake but are now a morass to be avoided by walkers except as spectacles to be viewed from above.

In addition, though both North Wales and Cumbria have suffered the depredations of industrial progress, North Wales has undoubtedly suffered more. One of its greatest lakes, Llyn Peris, was permanently scarred on its eastern shore by the massive spoil heaps of the Dinorwic Quarries in the eighteenth and nineteenth centuries, and at the moment of writing it is drained and practically nonexistent. For it is now to be changed further by becoming a reservoir in the latest pump-storage hydro-electric scheme in association with Llyn Marchlyn Mawr above on Elidir Fawr.

The effects of development like this are far reaching. Sometimes there is a much needed boost to local employment, but then a slump as the works are completed, leaving the local employment problem greater than before. Setting aside major environmental changes, small unseen factors also make their mark, which only time will reveal. For instance, what will happen to the *torgoch* (the Welsh char) which is thought to breed either in the river between Llyn Padarn and Peris, or in the shallows of Llyn Peris, neither of which at present exists?

Certain of the Forestry plantations do not enhance the lakes, though it must be said that no Welsh lake suffers as much from the serried files of the conifers as Ennerdale Water in the Lake District which I remember in my boyhood as a bare glaciated hollow much as the first prehistoric settlers and local farmers had left it. Now, sadly, both Wastwater and Ennerdale Water are under further threat.

Of course, the most historic human interest in the lakes has been in their utility. This is borne out by the way in which lakes are sometimes linked by a well-defined bridle path or drovers' road. Lakes provided natural watering places, with their own benison of precious forage on the way to and from them.

One of the most beautiful walks between two lakes is the old pack-horse route between Llynnau Tecwyn Isaf and Techwyn Uchaf. The lower and smaller of the two is one of the loveliest anywhere, with its population of Little Grebe, not quite inured to tourists in summer. The narrow bridle path to Llyn Tecwyn Uchaf rises behind the lake and the old paving flags over the boggy patches are soon evident.

Opposite Llyn Tecwyn Isaf

This is one of the oldest areas of settlement in Britain, with roads predating Roman and Saxon times, and the dwarf oak forest all round is predominantly native. The path rises through the ancient forest and into the more austere, humpy upland round Llyn Tecwyn Uchaf. The two lakes are connected by this old pack-horse route, for they have separate outflows direct to Traeth Bach. The view from either lake at sunset over this estuary is one of the glories of Wales.

From early times, lakes have been harnessed for either water supply or for power, and even corrie lakes high up on Yr Wyddfa, like Llyn Ffynnon-y-Gwas, have been harnessed to the needs of the quarries lower down. Much of this is by now industrial archaeology of course, the quarries being abandoned and the dams crumbling through the years.

There is a mystery about a captive sheet of water, whether it be some wide expansive lake like Llyn Tegid or a deep, enclosed quarry pool like Dorothea near Penygroes. Beneath the bland reflecting surface there is a life, or a death, beyond our comprehension: a nether world of another soft, but less yielding element, translucent rather than transparent; colourless, yet capable of holding greens and blues and blacks within its inscrutable embrace. What goes on beneath that surface is a mystery, so that men will sit for hours by its edge and, with expensive equipment and consummate skill and lore, will cast a hook and a float over it to catch a fish of a few ounces, perhaps wild little perch six inches long, whose exposed scarlet pectoral fins pulsating in the elaborate catch-net denote a sort of conquest of the mysterious and the inscrutable.

Even strangers immune to the hunting instinct will stand at the water's edge and ask how deep it is. Where the mystery seems especial, as at Llyn Glaslyn, the native's answer until quite recently would be 'bottomless'. And it would be believed, for how was the stranger, or even the native, to know? It *looked* bottomless. Quite a few of Snowdonia's lakes were pronounced 'bottomless' until the age of scientific enlightenment arrived, albeit a century or so later than elsewhere.

Llyn Ffynnon-y-Gwas

In 1900–01, Mr T. J. Jehu made soundings of the lakes of Snowdonia, and in 1902 his findings were published in the *Transactions of the Royal Society of Edinburgh* as 'Bathymetrical Survey of the Lakes of Snowdonia'. Mr Jehu may have supplied a statistic in answer to the inevitable question; he could not dissipate the mystery.

However, the deepest lake is Llyn Cowlyd, appropriately so, since Cowlyd is traditionally associated with that most mysterious of birds, the owl. Llyn Cowlyd has given soundings of 222 feet. At the other end of the scale, it will be no surprise to those who have climbed the shoulder of Yr-Ole-Wen and looked down into it that Llyn Ogwen is very shallow, with a mean depth of 6 feet and a maximum depth of only 10 feet.

And always, in all weathers and seasons, at all heights and whether at high noon or by moonlight, the lakes of Snowdonia have their special magic, a blend of geological origin, climate, natural life and human legend.

The major lakes are disposed in a roughly radial pattern, lying in directions north-west, north-east and south-west. The ridge running from Cnicht in the south-west to Moel Siabod in the north-east prevents any flow to the south-east. The three major north-west valleys run parallel, with from west to east Llyn Cwellyn, Llynnau Peris and Padarn and Llyn Ogwen. The south-west valley of Nant Gwynant holds Llynnau Gwynant and Dinas, while the north-east valleys run in four parallels, with from north to south Llynnau Eigiau, Cowlyd, Crafnant and Geirionydd.

Including the Llynnau Mymbyr at the centre of this radial pattern, that accounts for eleven major stretches of water enshrined in the dominant valleys of the Snowdon region. But in numerous hollows over the whole mountainous area are dotted lakes of varying extent and beauty. The best known of these are Llynnau Glaslyn and Llydaw under the east face of Snowdon and Llyn Idwal under the north face of Glyder Fawr. Depending on the definition of the word, there are some 150 lakes in North Wales. And they all belong to somebody. There is a common mis-apprehension among tourists in the National Park that the mountains and lakes belong to the nation, to themselves in fact, and this often leads to friction between the local farming community and their guests.

A farmer cannot be blamed, indeed should be supported, if he protests when he finds a visitor's dog running loose with sheep in lamb about. If he sees red when told that this is a National Park and belongs to 'us', is it any wonder? But it happens. Of course, it is not true that they belong to 'us'. Every mountain tract and lake has an owner, and even where the National Trust is the owner, it is not 'ours', but rather held in trust for us by an independent body.

There is a story I love about the late Sir Clough Williams-Ellis, when he was showing King George VI and the present Queen Mother round the area shortly after the war, and was describing to them the concept and parameters of the future National Park. Sharing the common misapprehension that it would soon belong to the public, His Majesty asked Sir Clough who owned a certain area he was indicating. 'I do,' replied Sir Clough, 'but you can keep that under your crown.'

It has to be remembered that any walker who wishes studiously to avoid the offence of trespass must keep to the public footpaths and bridleways. The only official record of these ways is the responsibility of the local county council, which is required by Act of Parliament to prepare and maintain a definitive map showing all bridleways, public footpaths and roads used as public footpaths.

Access to wild areas of countryside has been proceeding for quite some time, and the 'hiking' craze of the '30s, when ordinary working people decided to leave behind their run-down environment and 'up and off' into the hills, probably precipitated the Access to Mountains Act of 1939. But it was decimated by amendments. It took another decade and a war before a decent definition was made and enacted. The Access to the Countryside Act 1949 defines open countryside as 'mountain, moor, heath, down, cliff or foreshore', and excludes all agricultural land other than rough grazing.

For the hill and lake walker this can present difficulties, since it can inhibit spontaneity and even safety in choosing a route. The Ordnance Survey maps are useful since they indicate paths, and although not gospel may be taken as a fair guide to public ways. The latest edition on the new scale of 1 : 50,000 is not very reassuring on paths and can be frightfully vague.

But outside that, one can be guilty of trespass and some walkers, while zealous of maintaining public paths, can be guilty of straying across what they may think is common land but which in fact may be private land where sheep and lamb are being jealously herded by an anxious farmer.

It is amazing how the passage of, say, a score of walkers over a dry-stone wall can dislodge enough stones to allow sheep to stray. The importance of an intact wall is demonstrated by the sheep farmers' custom of having a flock that is *cynefin*: that is, one which is hereditary to that particular farmland, born to it for generations past. But a farmer cannot always maintain that and must buy sheep in as a result of disease or a drought year and so on. Only the most rigorous attention to walls and fences will keep these imported sheep from wandering, and they will wander for many miles, often beyond recovery. So that is a strict rule for

35

walkers: a stone off a wall must be replaced. But it is always better to use proper openings, rather than scaling the wall.

The word 'common' in reference to lands means common *rights*, not ownership. These rights may not always include walking rights. The land itself is still owned privately and the common rights referred to usually mean the ancient privileges to commoners to cut turf or firewood or to graze animals. In many cases common land has become the property of the local authority and footpaths have been provided.

The Forestry Commission and the National Trust, both large landowners, provide generous access, and Llyn Elsi and Llyn Idwal are only two examples. There are others where lakes and the land round them are privately owned, but where the owners do not object to access.

But access to the wilder areas where mountain lakes abound is not an automatic right. Common-sense and common courtesy are required of the walker who wishes to enjoy them to the full.

The lakes in the National Park are there to be enjoyed, never to be abused. One or two public bodies are in danger of abusing them and private individuals are occasionally guilty, especially in the way of litter. But by and large, the lakes remain as they were, given the prevailing changes of nature over the centuries, like the forest clearance, subsequent farming and afforestation. It is still possible to respond to them as Borrow did over a century ago when roads hardly existed and most of the people spoke Welsh only. 'Manifold were the objects which we saw from the brow of Snowdon', he wrote, 'but of all the objects which we saw, those which filled us with most delight and admiration, were numerous lakes and lagoons which, like ice or polished silver, lay reflecting the rays of the sun in deep valleys at our feet.'

One of the attractions of lake-walking in Snowdonia is that it can never really be completed. There are, as we have seen, some 150 lakes in the area, depending on the definition of the word 'lake'. In fact, if every permanent sheet of water were included, I have heard the figure 400 quoted, and I know from my own experience that this could be substantiated.

If you take, say, Llyn Conglog which hangs over the bend of the valley of Cwmorthin near Blaenau Ffestiniog, there are two or three small but quite separate tarns nearby. Yet the presence of Llyn Conglog, such a considerable lake hidden away on its surprising height, obscures these satellites. So where some walkers might quote three or four lakes here, for me there is only one, Llyn Conglog. Not that I ignore the satellites – but they remain mostly innominate and uncounted.

Even so, there must remain lakes I have not visited, perhaps shall never visit. There is even one quite large lake, Llyn Cynwch, quite easily accessible in the forest near Ganllwyd north of Dolgellau which I am well aware of (and have viewed from the summit of Cader Idris), but which I have left for some unspecified future date to visit. And even when I do, there will still be others, like Llyn Clyd, which feeds Llyn Idwal. I have seen Llyn Clyd from the heights above, but so far it has escaped my footsteps, if only because there is so much else of interest in the area.

Tiny Llyn Glas on Yr Wyddfa is much the same. And there is one, Llyn Pryfed, trapped by a hump against the crags of Craig Wion in a remote part of northern Ardudwy. It looks very interesting on the map and, like a miser, I am hoarding it. Yet it may be very dull, perhaps silting up – who knows? That is the thrill of searching out lakes, for while on the map they all appear as little blue patches, whether they be as deep as Llyn Dulyn or as silted as Llyn-y-Dywarchen under Moel Ysgyfarnogod, their individual character can only be measured by actually visiting them.

Waves and shingle: Llyn
Conglog

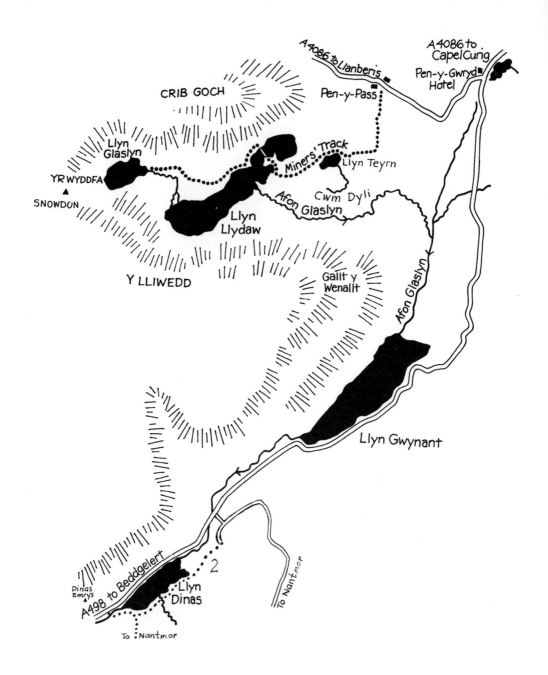

Two Glaslyn

Naturally, the best known lakes in North Wales are those associated with Yr Wyddfa (Snowdon) itself. Since Yr Wyddfa is the highest mountain in England and Wales, everybody wants to conquer it, so much so that human feet have become a noticeable erosion factor on the summit. Several systems of drainage radiate from the summit, but the most dramatic is that on the east side, where the Ice Age glacier collected the snows and tore its way down what is now Cwm Dyli, a deep U-shaped cwm all too apparent from the eastern approaches to Snowdon. Near Pen-y-Gwryd, the glacier then turned abruptly south-west, scooping out what is now Nant Gwynant.

660558

All the upper lakes, first Teyrn, then Llydaw and Glaslyn, are reached by the same route, the Miners' Track which heads west from the car park opposite Gorphwysfa Youth Hostel at Pen-y-Pass. It is a wide path, and the only real climb is between Llydaw and Glaslyn. Since Pen-y-Pass is at 1,169 feet above sea level, and Glaslyn, though among the highest lakes in North Wales, is just short of 2,000 feet, this amounts to a net climb of less than a thousand feet and is not nearly as rigorous as it may look on the map. The entire round trip from Pen-y-Pass should take no more than a couple of hours.

The Miners' Track is probably the most tramped mountain route in the country, so for those able to choose, it is better to ignore it during the holiday season and walk if possible on a sunny winter's day. As like as not, the peak of Yr Wyddfa will be covered with snow, conditions will be generally alpine and in a really cold snap the lakes will be frozen. The top lake, Llyn Glaslyn, is still easily reached, but unless you are kitted out for full winter hill-walking,

617546

lyn Teyrn, miners' track, Yr Wyddfa

it is better to let that suffice as the day's destination. Certainly winter is the best season to perceive the path of the glacier, whose course and remnants can be clearly traced. For a beginning, there is the steep slope of Snowdon's east face, first precipitous near the summit, then descending in a 45-degree angle of rock and scree into Llyn Glaslyn, all in front of your eyes as you ascend the Miners' Track to the lake, taking in Llyn Teyrn and Llyn Llydaw on the way. That east face is where the making of a cwm begins, and is nowhere more graphically demonstrated than with Llyn Glaslyn. The glacier descending from the peak tore with all its weight at the rock face, dragging erosive debris down the slope. The greatest erosion occurred at the bottom of the slope where it slowed up, scooping out an ice-filled basin and depositing a moraine of clay and boulders further on over an area of obtrusive rock whose hardness defied erosion. The build-up of this moraine at the lower end of the hollow accentuated the depth of the scooped-out area behind it, and at the ultimate melting of the ice left a depth sufficient to capture a lake of no great extent (less than quarter of a mile long) but of a much greater depth than the larger valley lakes lower down the system. Llyn Glaslyn is 127 feet deep, which seems remarkable considering its size. This scooping out, and the bare precipitous nature of the surrounding slopes, is what makes these corrie lakes so forbidding. On the hottest day in August I have never felt like bathing in Llyn Glaslyn. I suspect I am slightly afraid of it and although my rational side tells me I can drown in 6 feet as easily as in 120 feet once I am in difficulties, nevertheless nothing would induce me to be a devil and plunge into Glaslyn to cool off. Llyn Glaslyn was once known as Llyn Ffynnon Las – a name that has its origin in the lake's blue-green hue – Lake of the Blue Spring.

Llyn Glaslyn has been painted many times. The abstract quality of its mirror surface against the beetling crags all round, with the strident pyramid of Yr Wyddfa itself breaking into the sky behind, is perhaps what attracts artists. Here is the backdrop for the *Götterdämmerung*, and if I reach Glaslyn and pay it respects and then pass on, I can only say Glaslyn will look after itself and needs nobody to commend it. Darkly it sits below the summit, deceptively tranquil on a bright summer's day, but cruelly lashed by spume and waves when a January blizzard whiplashes over Bwlch-y-Saethau, the col between Lliwedd and Yr Wyddfa above the lake. Taking my glove off on one such day, my hand

41

stuck to the steel of my ice axe and, as we descended, the ice built up on our eyebrows to ludicrous proportions. Even so we had to help an incautious couple who had travelled to Snowdon on a moped and hoped to climb on such a day in thin shoes! At 1,970 feet above sea level, there are days when Glaslyn might be high on some Alpine flank. Bare rock between the ice-bands on the face of Lliwedd makes excellent Alpine and Himalayan conditions for the hardiest climbers.

This highest and most remote of the larger lakes abounds in legend. It is supposed that no bird will fly over it, that it is the abode of demons, that it is bottomless, that it never freezes and that it harbours no ordinary fish. How these legends spring up in the first place is the greatest mystery. The lake is not bottomless as we know, though in fairness it has to be said that soundings were not made till 1900–01, by T.J. Jehu. It certainly freezes, as I myself can testify. On January 10th, 1980, the strange patterns of ice forming were already evident after only a week of cold but not severe weather. Most climbers and walkers on Yr Wyddfa must have enjoyed the sight of ravens sailing in a great sweep over Glaslyn. I am prepared to concede that the demons emanate from the same *frisson* that affects me whenever I reach Glaslyn. As to harbouring no ordinary fish, the Carr and Lister appendix on 'The best fishing lakes in Snowdonia' lists Glaslyn as 'free' while under 'kind of fish' both Glaslyn and Llydaw warrant no more than a dash! Lockwood writes: 'Old local anglers speak of having caught large trout, but the washings from the copper mine must have killed them. The writer put a score of trout from Cwm-y-Ffynnon into Llyn Llydaw in 1912, on the east side of the causeway, and rises have been seen since.' But divers exploring the lake in the early 'fifties pronounced them dead.

The strangest legend of all concerns the afangc, a monster which inhabited the Beaver pool near Betws-y-Coed over twelve miles away to the east (incidentally, the Welsh beaver is *afanc*, but no matter, for the sake of the story). At any rate, this dreadful monster was secured by chains and drawn by a pair of oxen through Dolwyddelan parish and over the pass between Moel Siabod and Cribau, called Bwlch Rhiw-yr-Ychain (pass of the oxen's slope). One ox struggled so hard with the load that it lost an eye on the western slope, which was then called Gwaun Lygad yr Ych (field of the ox's eye), and its tears formed a pool – Pwll

Copper mine works: Llyn
Llydaw

Lygad yr Ych, which never dries up although no stream either
enters or flows out of it. The descent into 'Nant Gwynen' (no
doubt Nant Gwynant) proved easy after all that labour uphill, and
the monster was conveyed to Llyn Glaslyn without further
incident.

The outflow from Llyn Glaslyn is quite as dramatic as the lake
itself. The stream plunges over rocky shelves to Llyn Llydaw
below. Llyn Llydaw spreads *across* the direction of the stream and
the exit is not at the end of its long axis but at the south-east side,
where it falls steeply into Cwm Dyli.

Llyn Llydaw, at 1,455 feet, by contrast with the loneliness of Glaslyn has an industrial, used air about it; the Miners' Track crosses its eastern end by a causeway and the ruins of a crushing mill lie nearby. The causeway was built in 1853 when the lake was lowered. A slate panel commemorates its completion thus:

> This causeway was built by the Cwm Dyli Rock and Green Lake Copper Mining Company under the direction of the mining captain, Thomas Colliver. During its construction the level of the lake was lowered 12 feet and 6,000 cubic yards of waste rock from the mine were used to build the embankment. The causeway was first crossed on October 13th 1853.

Remembering that all that rock was hewn and hauled by manual labour, Captain Thomas Colliver can have been no easy task master.

Causeway: Llyn Llydaw

I talked recently to Mr J. Morgan of Nant Peris, who worked in the Glaslyn copper mine as a boy till its closure in 1915 'on account of the war taking all the men'. He worked five and a half days a week at one shilling a day, with fourpence an hour for overtime. They lived in the barracks by the side of Llyn Llydaw; 'the Beddgelert Barracks was higher up'. I was intrigued by this evidence of apartheid, for local rivalries were quite intense in those days. It has to be remembered that the Llanberis Pass had not been opened for more than two generations. At noon on Saturday they all left for home and on Sunday evening they would assemble in Nant Peris for the long walk back to their barracks: 'If we got there,' Mr Morgan told me; 'because there was sometimes a lot of fighting on the way.' First man to return had to light the fire and put the big iron boiler on, to brew the tea. Thereafter the fire was kept alight for the whole week, and two men were deputed each night to get up to stoke it up. High jinks took the form of strewing holly leaves in the path of the poor bare-footed night-watchman who got up to do his stint at the fire.

The ore was carried by overhead cable in buckets from Llyn Glaslyn (or Llyn Glas, as Mr Morgan insisted on calling it) to the smelter on Llyn Llydaw. 'We weren't supposed to swim or drink water from the lakes. It gave you a sore throat. But if you did and you had your sore throat, you might as well drink the whole lake for all the harm it would do you. . . .'

It says something for the strength imbued by this hardy early life that while I was in Nant Peris, this old gentleman shinned up by extension ladder and rope to the belfry of the old church to mend the bell-rope. The bell, I noticed, dated 1630.

Llydaw is deeper still than Glaslyn, 190 feet all told, and larger. It was on the shores of Llydaw that the copper ore from the Glaslyn mine was crushed and as a result of this it is recorded that in 1899 the waters of Llydaw first assumed their present greenish hue. The lake spread across the cwm, held back by an enormous rock barrier and all round there is evidence of glacier drift.

The dominant bird over lakes like Llydaw is the herring gull and it is interesting to note an ecological change since Pennant's time. In 1784, Pennant recorded of the Great Black-backed gulls on Llydaw that they 'broke the silence of this sequestered place by their deep screams'. There is no sign of the Great Black-backed gull now and the ubiquitous herring gull has learned to live by a well rewarded parasitism on tourists all the way up Yr Wyddfa and increasingly towards the summit where they have become so tame as to walk almost over your feet. No bird can ever arouse resentment in me, but I find the herring gull a thorough bore, and when on some remote lake I find Pennant's shyer Black-backed, I am delighted.

641548 Just east of Llydaw and lower down the side of Cwm Dyli is another scooped out hollow wherein Llyn Teyrn lies just below the Miners' Track. I have no idea why this smallest of the three lakes in Cwm Dyli should bear such a princely name – *Teyrn* means monarch.

Llyn Teyrn

E. W. Steeple writes:

> This lake is one of the three in the Snowdonia hills which Llwyd refers to as 'bearing names which have puzzled the best criticks in the British'. I have heard of no tradition connecting it with any particular personage, but if we regard it as having been a sort of royal fish pond the name presents no real difficulty, as the Beddgelert valley figures largely in Welsh folklore as the home of princes.

But one interesting fact emerged when Llydaw was lowered to make a causeway. Llydaw has always had Arthurian associations and Arthur, according to Welsh tradition, met his death in a skirmish at Bwlch-y-Saethau. When the waters of Llydaw were lowered, a primitive canoe, hollowed out of a solid oak trunk, was found embedded in the mud. It measured about ten feet long by two and a half feet wide. Richenda Scott in *Snowdonia* writes:

> . . . looking down from the heights into the dark waters of the lake, Sir John Rhys saw 'with the eyes of Mallory' the passing of Arthur enacted on its waters, the reluctant Sir Bedivere flinging Excalibur into the depths below, and the 'barge' transformed into the prehistoric canoe, containing the three 'fayre ladyes' who bore away the body of the mortally wounded king, staunching his wounds.

But the canoe probably confirms a long history of settlement on Llyn Llydaw. It seems to have been of a type almost invariably associated with lake dwelling. Now Llydaw is the Welsh for Armorica, and Pugh translates it as 'extending along the water', and Stokes as 'coastland', from which Sir John Rhys assumes that it was probably the name of a lake settlement, traces of which he believes seem to substantiate this here.

The outflow from Llyn Llydaw into the higher reaches of Nant Gwynant is steep, steep enough to attract the attention of the engineers who captured the waters in a pipe-line to feed the turbines in the power-house on the floor of Nant Gwynant.

653540

Llyn Gwynant

The old name for the vale was Nanhwynen or Nan-Hwynan. It used to be more heavily wooded and Edward Llwyd wrote: 'At Nanhwynein trees were so thick that a man on a white horse could not be seen from Llyn Dinas to Pen-y-Gwryd, except in two places, and one of these has ever since been called Goleugoed' (literally, 'Lightwood'). And today, at a point not far below the top of the pass where the road crosses a little stream, the bridge, more a culvert, is called Pont Goleugod.

645520

Nant Gwynant is a long valley, some seven miles long, and its two valley lakes are among Snowdonia's best. The first, Llyn Gwynant, is about three miles from the head of the valley. A flat expanse of meadowland stretching about a mile above the lake suggests it was once much longer. The lake is firmly locked into its part of the valley by the encroaching hills at its foot, and the outflow runs through these hills for about one and a half miles to Dinas. This narrow glen, especially in winter, has the austerity of tone and colour reminiscent of a Chinese landscape painting. This feeling gets stronger lower down, as we shall see.

49

Winding down the valley by the road from Pen-y-Gwryd there are superb views of Llyn Gwynant below and up into Cwm Dyli on the right. The lake is very beautiful, perhaps the most picturesque in Snowdonia. It is especially fine when seen with Moel Hebog as background in the westering sun.

On the roadside, the little beaches of gravel by the lake are usually fully occupied by tourists in summer. Across the lake, a great bastion of rock rises out of the water, with above, the flanks of Gallt-y-Wenallt rising steeply for nearly two thousand feet.

The Chinese quality I have mentioned was noticed in the late 'fifties by film maker Mark Robson when he was shooting the well-known *Inn of the Sixth Happiness*. One of the spoil-heaps of the old copper mines below Dinas was employed for a village sequence and convincingly portrayed a bareness and poverty suitable for the general background of the film. Even more touching was the use of Llyn Dinas itself.

Llyn Dinas

Miss Ingrid Bergman in the role of Miss Gladys Aylward the missionary, fleeing from the advancing Japanese, arrived at a 'river' with her schoolchildren; they were conveyed across on a makeshift raft. In reality they embarked near the boathouse at the lower end of Llyn Dinas and landed on the boulder-strewn shore at the other side and were then able to trek on to salvation over lower hills and ultimately to a flatland which was a low-angle view down Traeth Bach with Ynys Gifftan rising beneficently out of the horizon. I confess that the memory of that film has ever since coloured my view of Llyn Dinas and its environment. I prefer it in winter when the tones are muted and the sparse grasses and boulders of its shoreline are seen at their best. I have no direct acquaintance with China, but I am forcibly reminded of certain Chinese paintings whenever I walk round Llyn Dinas. Perhaps it is the old weathered bole of a dead oak near the foot of the lake, contrasting with a very lively and ornamental pine, which colours my meditations, as though it were all pointing to some allegory of life and death.

617495   Llyn Dinas is fairly shallow with a mean depth of 13 feet and a maximum depth of 30 feet. There is ample evidence, of course, of silting and the lake was probably once much deeper. The Afon Goch, which flows into the south side, would be a contributory factor, for in a wet spell it is quite a cascade.

606493   Llyn Dinas, no less than the upper lakes, has its legend, though possibly with more foundation in fact. Votigern, a sort of fifth column Welshman, allowed the Saxons in to assist him in his quarrels with local Welsh neighbours and with the Picts. Legend has it that he tried to build a castle on the crag above Llyn Dinas, just downstream on the right, but he was defeated by local magic, the foundations disappearing each night. Myrddin Emrys (Merlin of the Arthurian cycle) was among the miscreants and when Vortigern finally threw in the sponge and left in royal dudgeon, Myrddin Emrys moved in and occupied the fortress for some time, hence its name Dinas Emrys. Aurelius Ambrosius, a man with a proper sense of Roman *gravitas*, then sought out Myrddin Emrys and persuaded him to leave with him as his adviser and soothsayer. Before leaving, Myrddin buried his treasure within the fortress. Naturally, the place has been dug over and indeed some lesser 'treasure' has been found: twelve stud nails of bronze with traces of gold plating, probably used for riveting armour, and some iron terrets coated with bronze, used on harness.

Icing on Llyn Llydaw

Below the lake the River Glaslyn flows over an ice-deepened floor of rock, constricted by encroaching hills on either side, thus providing the most beautiful water-course in Snowdonia, past Dinas Emrys and the meadows above Beddgelert (once a lake) down through the dramatic gorge of Aberglaslyn and thence on over flat marshland to Porthmadog and the sea.

The walks round the south side of Llyn Dinas and up its southern flanks are among the best in the area, with superb views of the lake from the steep path that rises from the foot of the lake and over the flank of Moel Dyniewyd to Nantmor.

613477

The entire Glaslyn system is a classical example of glacial action and all five lakes – Glaslyn, Llydaw, Teyrn, Gwynant and Dinas – demonstrate the various conditions that contribute to the formation of lakes. The cirque lake of Glaslyn right under the summit of Yr Wyddfa, the corrie lakes of Llydaw and Teyrn hanging over the main valley, and the two elongated valley lakes of Gwynant and Dinas with their alluvial silting, all result from the former action of the glacier and its subsequent melting.

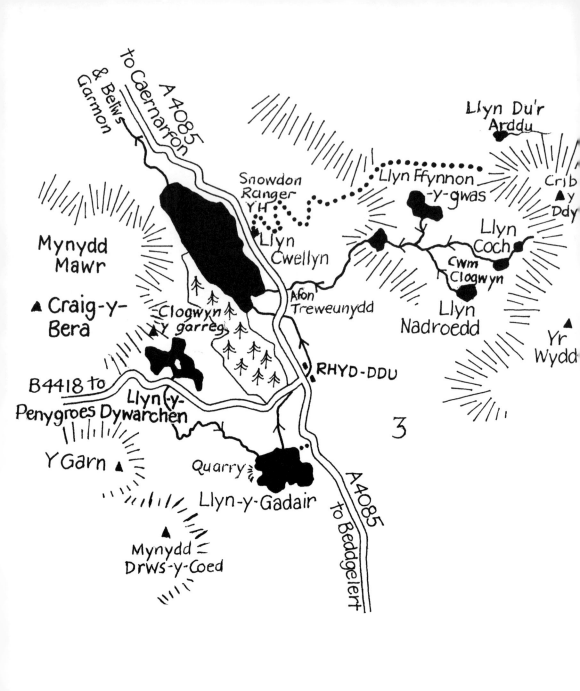

Three   Cwellyn

595545   The west face of Yr Wyddfa, like the east, is mostly sheer cliff. It drains first into a group of small corrie lakes in Cwm Clogwyn under the black crags of Llechog, thence by the steeply falling stream of Afon Treweunydd to Llyn Cwellyn. But those upper corrie lakes constitute quite a system on their own. Right under the summit itself the black corrie lakes of Llyn Nadroedd and Llyn Goch drain out of Cwm Clogwyn to a small innominate reservoir. Further north Llyn Ffynnon-y-gwas, also an old reservoir, drains into the same little reservoir. A small and endearing complex of old sheepfolds stands near the north shore of Ffynnon-y-gwas.

565551   A zig-zag path leads up from Snowdon Ranger Youth Hostel on the shores of Llyn Cwellyn to Llyn Ffynnon-y-gwas, with a view over to the other corrie lakes, and proceeds on to the shoulder between Crib-y-Ddysgl and the summit. From Cwellyn to the summit is a climb of over 3,000 feet so it constitutes a full day's walk with an early start, though none of it is difficult.

The view from this shoulder embraces not only all this upper Snowdon system but in the distance Llynnau Gadair, Nantlle, Dywarchen and Cwellyn. Llyn-y-Gadair, in particular, takes on a majesty it may not always possess close at hand, especially when the sun sinks behind Moel Hebog and its outliers.

560550   But for Llyn Cwellyn itself, the major lake in this system, the best approach is the road taken by Borrow from the Caernarfon direction. There is no great awareness of height on the seven mile ascent from Caernarfon to Cwellyn, which lies at 463 feet near the head of the pass over to Beddgelert. But there is drama. Leaving

Betws Garmon, the mountains gradually close in. 'The valley terminates in a deep gorge', says Borrow, 'between Eilio – which by the bye is part of the chine of Snowdon – and Pen Drws Coed. The latter, that couchant elephant with its head turned to the north-east, seems as if it wished to bar the pass with its trunk; by its trunk I mean a kind of jaggy ridge which descends to the road.' He is talking rather of Mynydd Mawr, one of the less glaciated masses of Snowdonia. The ridge does indeed descend precipitously into the lower end of the lake, providing a fine backdrop to a view across the lake from the road, and it is not stretching the imagination to see it from Betws Garmon as 'that couchant elephant'.

Llyn Cwellyn

The road alongside Cwellyn dates back at least to Roman times, connecting Segontium (Caernarfon) with a small station at Tremadog. That might sound unremarkable enough until one remembers that it was the only north–south pass through the mountains until the early part of the nineteenth century when the Llanberis Pass was opened by the miners. It is terrible to contemplate that the first miners working the copper in Cwm Dyli under the summit of Yr Wyddfa had to carry the ore on their backs over the shoulder of the mountain and down the other side to Llyn Cwellyn, from where it was transferred by pack-horse to Caernarfon. So Cwellyn at the end of the eighteenth century was more than a beautiful lake admired by visitors like Cradock and Pennant, but was the scene of a traffic in hard labour if ever that term meant anything.

The precipitous mound of Castell Cidwm dominates the lower end of Llyn Cwellyn. Legend has it that a wicked chieftain Cidwm shot a fatal arrow at the son of Queen Elen of the Hosts, who was leading her army through Eryri from South Wales. Since South Walians have always been called *hwntwrion* (outsiders or foreigners) by North Walians, the good queen seems to have been looking for trouble.

Borrow's interlocutor in reply to the inevitable questions about the depth of the lake and its fish was right. It is deep, 122 feet, and it is well known for its fish. William Williams in 1802 said that it held 'besides the common trout, those red-bellied Alpine trout, called char, which are in season about Christmas'. This fish has always aroused the interest of naturalists and anglers through the ages. Firstly, it is rare, found only in North Wales, and there only in four lakes: Llynnau Peris, Mymbyr, Bodlyn and Cwellyn. Two travellers, Ray and Willoughby, reported in the 1690s the local legend that the *torgoch* (literally 'red-belly') had been introduced from Rome by 'three sons of the church'. One cannot help wondering how they kept the creatures alive over that long journey. Defoe mentions the *torgoch*. And travellers in the past have always mentioned it in connection with Cwellyn. But sadly Mr Brymer Roberts of Llanberis reported that it was extinct in Cwellyn by 1946. Ray and Willoughby place the *torgoch* as the same as the alpine 'roetal' of the Continent, and this seems to be the right attribution, for the *torgoch* likes the cold alpine conditions of the deeper lakes.

Craig-y-Bera from Llyn-y-Dywarchen

545534

On all counts then, Cwellyn has been popular through the ages. It lives up to its reputation. Beyond the head of the lake Craig-y-Bera rises as a pure cone before the land falls to the pass of Drws-y-Coed over to Cwm Nantlle. The afforestation on the lower mounds at the head of the lake seems to enhance it. The view to the left and south-west from the lake embraces the heights of Yr Wyddfa from Clogwyn to the summit.

The Snowdon Ranger Youth Hostel stands half-way along the shore. It was here that Borrow met the original Snowdon Ranger and his son-in-law, a miner, and was so entranced by them and by Cwellyn that he stopped for one of his long and inimitable wayside chats. How deftly he captures in a few sentences the old man's pride in his work as he offers to guide Borrow up Snowdon. 'I would show your honour the black lake in the frightful hollow in which fishes have monstrous heads and little bodies, the lake on which neither swan, duck nor any kind of wildfowl was ever seen to alight. Then I would show your honour the fountain of the hopping creatures, where, where . . .'

He must have been a natural-born salesman, but Borrow had to press on to Beddgelert and so resisted the invitation. The Snowdon Ranger was right about his route being the best ascent to Snowdon and the cwm lakes that feed Cwellyn but the creatures, surely, are yet more anglers' tales!

Further along on the Beddgelert road there are two more lakes. Llyn-y-Gadair is a mile and a half on from Cwellyn. The pass here flattens out before a slight climb and then falls to Beddgelert. Without immediate crags to set it off, Llyn-y-Gadair is best seen on a calm evening with the sun setting behind the Mynydd Drws-y-Coed. If lakes, for the romantic, have an aesthetic function, then Llyn-y-Gadair's is to act as mirror. It is an angler's lake. Boats are tied up in little creeks cut out of the peat and here and there the ruins of clinker-built craft mark a long tradition of angling. There is no boathouse, but at the side farthest from the road there are the ruins of an old quarry works and the spoil spreads into the lake, fortunately not on a sufficient scale to offend the eye. This is part of the Cambrian slate band which stretches nearly twelve miles from Nantlle over to Dinorwic and Bethesda. Old quarries on the left of the road, Rhyd-ddu, Glanrafon and Ffridd are further evidence of the former industrial activity of the area. Now, not one quarry is working and the present business is seasonal tourism, for the car park at Rhyd-ddu is the starting point of one of the most popular routes up Snowdon. I notice that, among the slate flags laid down to ease the public path across boggy land between the road and Llyn-y-Gadair, there is one piece of slate ten feet long, evidence that it came out in good lengths, although the breadth may have been wanting for good roofing slates. A 'Princess', for instance, is 14 inches wide, though this is one of the larger sizes.

On a quiet day, the surface of Llyn-y-Gadair is ruffled only by the little wakes of grebe darting about for food. Walking round the lake is not exactly encouraged – as I say, it is an angler's lake and walkers and anglers do not mix easily.

560534 Llyn-y-Dywarchen, the lake that feeds Llyn-y-Gadair, is even more private – with warning notices everywhere. I remember enjoying this privacy to the full when I was one of a party invited by the owner to picnic on a long hot summer's day by its shore. This is a beautiful lake and we swam and exulted in utter peace. It has a small island, one of many igneous outcrops, *roches moutonnées*, in a highly glaciated area. A larger outcrop, Clogwyn-y-Garreg, rises steeply from the lakeside on the Nantlle side, a sentinel guarding the pass. Beyond, to the right of the pass the rugose crags and scree of Craig-y-Bera rise majestically with, on the other side, the dark north-facing precipice of Y Garn. The grass all round the lake is bitten close by sheep. There are no trees other than some small native scrub. The lake is complex in shape and has been deepened by the construction of a dam near the roadside.

Island: Llyn-y-Dywarchen

Once upon a time Dywarchen had a floating island which aroused the curiosity of Giraldus Cambrensis as early as 1188. He spoke of the lake 'having a floating island in it which is driven from one side to the other by the force of the wind'. Naturally that became a legend, but Giraldus had a perfectly rational explanation in an age of unquestioning faith: 'A part of the bank naturally bound together by the roots of willows and other shrubs may have broken off and being continually agitated by the winds . . . it cannot reunite itself firmly with the banks.'

In 1698 the astronomer Halley, with a scientist's proper scepticism, swam out to the island to verify that it did indeed float.

Cradock in 1770 tells how the local guides 'related many singular and surprising tales' about the lake and its island, and he indulged their credulity so far as to go and inspect it. He was not impressed. He found 'the lake as they called it was somewhat bigger than a duck-pond, and the island was a knotty piece of Bog which, after very heavy rains, might very possibly float in it'!

A little later, in 1784, Pennant claimed to have seen it and confirmed the story that cattle which strayed upon it when it was near the shore were occasionally marooned when it began to move. Alas, the floating island and its legends are now gone, unless another 'knotty piece of Bog' detaches itself.
But that is not quite the end of the mystery of Llyn-y-Dywarchen, for there was once another lake directly behind it, Llyn Bwlch-y-Moch, which appears on Ordnance Survey maps as recently as the 1962 edition, and not on other maps, depending on the date. Odder still, the first Ordnance Survey at the beginning of the nineteenth century shows no Llyn Bwlch-y-Moch.

The mystery is explained by examining the head and foot of Llyn-y-Dywarchen. They have been reversed by man. Llyn-y-Dywarchen occupies the actual watershed between the Cwellyn and the Nantlle system. When the first Ordnance Survey was plotted, Llyn-y-Dywarchen was probably shallower and more marshy (this explains Cradock's refusal to be impressed) and drained off into the valley of Bwlch-y-Moch which winds in an almost complete circle round the bastion of Clogwyn-y-Garreg. From there it is drained off by the Afon Llyfni into Cwm Nantlle;

Dam at Bwlch-y-Moch

Overleaf Llyn-y-Dywarchen
from Bwlch-y-Moch

in other words, in the opposite direction to its present outflow into Llyn-y-Gadair. I would guess that in dry weather, Bwlch-y-Moch was a flat marshy bottom of bog myrtle and fescue pasture and that only in a wet season was it in any sense a lake. Certainly there are still signs of a shoreline. But this fluctuation would present a problem of whether or not to mark the lake and the first Survey decided against it.

Then an earth dam was built at the narrow exit from Llyn-y-Dywarchen, closing off the flow into Cwm Bwlch-y-Moch. A stone-faced dam was built at the other end, near the road, and the level of Llyn-y-Dywarchen thus raised sufficiently to enable it to spill over into the Cwellyn system by flowing through a sluice in the dam to Llyn-y-Gadair. So the flow of Llyn-y-Dywarchen has been completely reversed over the years in the cause of water supply and angling, and Bwlch-y-Moch has consequently become even drier. But man's interference has enhanced Llyn-y-Dywarchen, and by no means could it be described as 'somewhat bigger than a duck-pond'.

Just below the little dam at the back of Llyn-y-Dywarchen, a ruined *bwthyn* (cottage) stands under a group of weather-worn sycamores, on the edge of what was once Llyn Bwlch-y-Moch. There are the ruins of outhouses too. Did they once keep pigs here? No evidence that I can see tells us that they did, though the outhouses have in an intersecting wall a low aperture which would fit those low-slung domestic beasts. Or does the name refer to the hog-back profile of Clogwyn-y-Garreg from Cwm Nantlle? Or does it refer to the vicissitudes of Lleu Llaw Gyffes in the ancient tale of the *Mabinogion* where a boar guides Gwydion to Nantlle in search of Lleu?

Naturally, since Llyn Bwlch-y-Moch is now dry, it is tempting to abandon it, but it is worth skirting the bastion of Clogwyn-y-Garreg to explore the extent of the former lake. It must have been a splendid bow-shape. At its foot, there is ample evidence that it was once an important source of energy for the old copper-works below in Cwm Nantlle, because there are the remains of a handsomely built stone dam. The masonry is of dressed granite blocks, with stone-faced sluices. The centre of the structure has been dismantled to ensure that water is no longer held back, and given that fishermen are forever searching for waters, I wonder why. Llyn Bwlch-y-Moch could soon be restored by resuscitating the dam and another glorious stretch of water well hidden from the road by Clogwyn-y-Garreg would once again provide fishermen with aquatic territory, if that is not an oxymoron.

And the once splendid dam explains why the first Ordnance Survey did not show any lake. The lake existed only after the dam was built (after 1840), to serve the mines. According to the 1962 map it was still in existence (long after the closure of the mines), after which the breaching of the dam once again drained it.

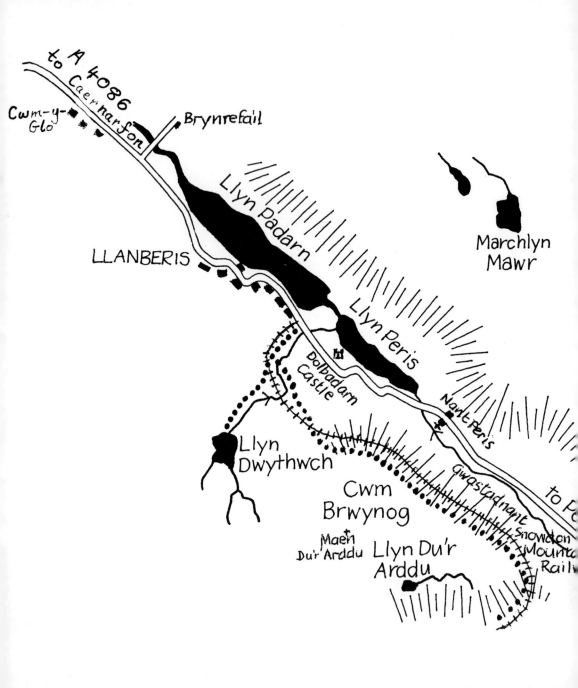

Four Llanberis

The most dramatic glaciated valley in the area is the Llanberis Pass. Until the beginning of the nineteenth century there was no road through it, and it must have been quite a tortuous ascent 648556 from either side to what is now the Pen-y-Pass Youth Hostel at the actual watershed, because the whole valley is strewn with glacial debris and erratic blocks perch on the edge of cliffs all down the slopes. One enormous block was recently blown up to facilitate road widening, not without protest, since every block is beloved by climbers and tourists. The road was first made in about 1830 by the copper miners on Yr Wyddfa, enabling them to transport their ore by the well-known Miners' Track first to Pen-y-Pass (Gorphwysfa), then down the Nant Peris side and along the flat valley floor to Caernarfon.

This flattening out is so noticeable as to earn a specific Welsh 610580 name, *Gwastadnant* – literally, 'the smooth level valley'. There are superb climbing pitches on either side of Gwastadnant.

But until the road was built, the old church of Nant Peris could only be reached by water from Cwm-y-Glo, so that Llyn Padarn was quite a commercial waterway around the time of the Industrial Revolution, when the mining companies were so busy in these parts. In the mid-eighteenth century, the presiding genius of this waterway was an Amazon by the name of Margaret Ferch Evan of Penllyn who carried, in boats of her own building, the ore produced by the Nant Peris copper mine and delivered it at Cwm-y-Glo. Pennant, who heard of her fame when she was ninety, described her as 'the greatest hunter, shooter and fisher of her time, a relentless foe to the foxes of Snowdonia, a breeder of dogs, a musician and a wrestler'.

67

593593
575613

In the flat area at the foot of the pass lie the two famous lakes of Llyn Peris and Llyn Padarn. When the glacier melted there must have been one long lake nearly five miles long. But alluvial drifting at the foot of the pass around Nant Peris filled the head of the lake, while debris from Afon Llwch eventually dissected the lake with an encroaching delta, so that now there are two major lakes at the same altitude – 340 feet above sea level.

Oddly enough, Llyn Peris, which is the upper lake, is the deeper (or was – more on that later) at 114 feet, while Padarn, which is the larger, is rather shallower at 94 feet.

At the time of writing, Llyn Peris is a tragic eyesore. What was once one of Wales's most significant lakes has been given over to the Central Electricity Generating Board for a pump-storage scheme in tandem with Llyn Marchlyn Mawr high above over the flank of Elidir Fawr. A vast tunnel will connect the two. Huge machines with names like 'Iron Fairy', bulldozers, grabs and enormous tippers manoeuvre about the floor of the lake which has been drained. On the far side, the same machinery traverses the great slate tips of Dinorwic Quarries, but there they are Lilliputian in the vast scale of the terraces where throughout the last century and half-way through this one, local quarrymen worked the colossal hillside terraces.

Aesthetically, this is a major disaster area. One artist/climber friend of mine who made his modest living in the area has moved on to Scotland as though from some contagion. In the same circumstances, I would have done the same. But I am fortunate in living on Traeth Bach, where the only development is Portmeirion, and that at least is fun.

Considering Llyn Peris was one of the major lakes in Wales, its proposed use was a classical environmental issue. It was not the first in the area. I well remember, shortly after the war, listening to Lord Birkett speaking out-of-doors near Llyn Ogwen when several large hydro-electric schemes were mooted for North Wales. Without this sort of protest from people who care for the preservation of our landscape, it is possible that by now many of Snowdonia's corrie lakes would have been deepened by dams and hydro-electric schemes would dot every valley. Instead, we have kept our valleys fairly intact, though we have two atomic power stations in North Wales, with the threat of a nuclear dust-bin somewhere in the mountains always in our ears.

There is a serious moral choice here, very much concerned with the world energy crisis. I am an ardent and convinced environmentalist, but I am uncomfortably aware that until we find alternatives to fossil fuel energy, the present choice lies mainly between hydro-electric and nuclear schemes. I live seven miles from an atomic station and I hope its like will not proliferate in North Wales. But that can only be if other people put up with them – or we have a great deal more hydro-electric schemes. If the latter is the only alternative to nuclear stations, then Snowdonia will be a prime target eventually and this book could be a celebration of something that will disappear in its present, mostly natural state.

This is no place to argue the point, merely, in relation to Llyn Peris, to point out the alternatives. Of course, like everybody else I live in hope of some tremendous breakthrough in solar, wind or tidal energy, but I confess I see little immediate hope there and as things stand between now and the end of the century, Lyn Peris will be only the first of several such schemes as demand for electric power increases and fossil fuels, particularly oil, become either scarce or prohibitive in price.

For anybody interested in the sheer scale of modern earth-moving technology, Llyn Peris must be fascinating. I confess to being horrified and must record merely that the scale is Cyclopean. What it will all be like in the end, I do not know, and I would not doubt that the engineers aim to restore the lake to some of its former beauty when it is filled again. If it is like the smaller Llyn Stwlan pump-storage scheme on the Moelwyns, it will mean that the upper lake, Llyn Marchlyn Mawr, will be emptied downhill during peak demand on the national grid, thus raising the level of Llyn Peris (and Llyn Padarn too, unless Peris is to be dammed at its lower end). At off-peak periods, the water will be pumped back up to Marchlyn Mawr, from surplus power produced by nuclear means.

So such a scheme depends on the nuclear boost for pumping the water back uphill. Llyn Peris will then have tides, so to speak, with the inevitable tidemark, which is always unsightly in lakes, as for instance during protracted droughts like 1976. If this is the price we must pay to minimize the proliferation of nuclear power stations, then we must have no illusions about it. Pump storage schemes in any case are only viable in association with surplus production at atomic stations during off-peak periods. It seems that we are about to expand our nuclear programme to such an extent that the Llyn Peris scheme will become a drop in the ocean. If that be so, then I believe the scheme is the precursor of one of the major environmental disasters of the century.

It has to be said, however, that the Dinorwic Quarries had already done their worst for Llyn Peris, for the scale of the quarries above the eastern shore, and the sheer volume of waste tipping into the lake, have to be seen to be believed. The nineteenth century was perhaps slower in pace than ours, but it was no less ruthless and massive in its production and pollution. Aberfan and Llyn Peris are the two major examples in Wales.

Llyn Peris

Yet I have always remembered Llyn Peris as possessing its own dark beauty and the trees on the western shore with the old castle of Dolbadarn on its knoll between the two lakes have always enhanced it. Looking along the shore, and taking full advantage of the castle's romantic profile, nineteenth-century water-colourists and print-makers made it one of Britain's most celebrated views.

Since the eighteenth century, Llyn Peris has always had its share of industry. All along the pass there were copper mines and the mining company's stamping mill, employing about a hundred boys, was at the end of the lake. At its height, towards the end of the last century, Dinorwic Quarry was the biggest slate quarry in the world, employing 3,000 men. It had its own foundry, and every machine that was brought in was first stripped down so that each part could be duplicated, thus ensuring that breakdowns were kept to the minimum.

Much of this foundry is preserved as an industrial museum. Among the moving parts in the quarry system was the largest water-wheel in the world (Dinorwic seems to have anticipated the *Guinness Book of Records* by many years). With a diameter of 50 feet, it is still there for visitors to admire. The output of the quarry in 1880 was 20,000 tons, and by 1898 it had reached no less than 485,000 tons. I have no information on this as a relative performance, but my guess is that it was the largest in the world!

A narrow-gauge railway carried the finished slate products to Portdinorwic, six miles away. Two miles of this track have been resuscitated to provide a lakeside ride by the shore of Llyn Padarn.

Llyn Padarn by contrast has traditionally been a tourist centre with fine Victorian hotels in the village of Llanberis. During his journey in North Wales with his friends the Thrales in 1774, Dr Samuel Johnson visited Llanberis. The nearest he got to the mountains was Dolbadarn Castle, 'to which we climbed with great labour. I was breathless and harassed.' For anticlimactic hyperbole, this must compete with Henry James who, after climbing a hill in Wessex with views over five counties, said: 'How perfectly jolly!' – or with Sir Edmund Hillary coming down after the first ascent of Everest and greeting his jubilant companions with, I believe, 'Well, we knocked the old bugger off.'

There used to be a branch railway from Caernarfon to Llanberis, so that the journey from London or the Midlands usually involved only one change. Now, Bangor is the nearest station, but the tourist industry continues to flourish in Llanberis.

Llanberis is the base for the Snowdon Mountain Railway, and in summer the lake and the village swarm with visitors. But Llyn Padarn is large enough (two miles long) and the amenities sufficient in number and quality to absorb them. A new Environmental Centre is in the process of construction at the edge of the lake.

Dotted round the village are a number of small industries, and if they do not exactly enhance the area, they do provide employment in what, since the demise of the slate industry, has been a depressed region.

Access to the lake has been made easier by the construction of a by-pass (more or less along the track of the old branch railway line) which runs along the western shore, providing a sort of esplanade. Across the water the little quarrymen's cottages sit low on the rocky slopes, almost unchanged for a century or more.

Over the lake's outflow there is a fine arched bridge, which offers a magnificent view beyond the full length of the lake to the mountain flanks of the pass rising into the clouds, plane after plane in constantly changing light when there is cloud about. It is one of those resplendent views when even the wettest day provides drama with clouds coming over the peaks and falling into the valley. One of the most memorable sights of Llyn Padarn was arranged in 1958 when the sculling events of the Commonwealth Games were held there. The needle-like craft skimming over the silken surface of the lake have remained in my mind as one of those images that are never repeated in life.

Before leaving Llyn Padarn, of course it would be sacrilege not to mention that the *torgoch* is (or was) found in both Padarn and Peris. Although I am only a lay naturalist and even less of an angler, I am delighted to record that at 11 a.m. on November 8th, 1979, as I was standing in heavy rain on the old bridge over Llyn Padarn's outflow, watching the pattern of the rain lashing the lake's surface, there leapt with a flash of silver and red out of the water the unmistakable *torgoch*.

Given these two major valley lakes, it is surprising how few small mountain tarns there are associated with the Llanberis system. Almost directly above Llyn Peris on the south-west slopes there is a small corrie lake, Llyn Dwythwch, whose only claim to fame seems to have been its mention in a survey of 1352, where it was noted as contributing to the wealth of the manor of Dolbadarn with its fishing.

High up under the crags of Clogwyn Du'r Arddu on the northern flank of Yr Wyddfa, and only visible from the Llanberis and Snowdon Ranger paths, lies the tiny lake of Llyn Du'r Arddu which trickles out into Afon Arddu down the long Cwm Brwynog towards Llyn Peris. Not far below it lies one of the largest isolated boulders in Snowdonia with the distinctive name of Maen Du'r Arddu. From the shoulder above Cwm Brwynog there is a superb prospect northwards to Llyn Padarn far below.

But beyond many a pool that hardly qualifies, that is the sum of the lakes in the Llanberis system.

601558

Old bridge: Llyn Padarn

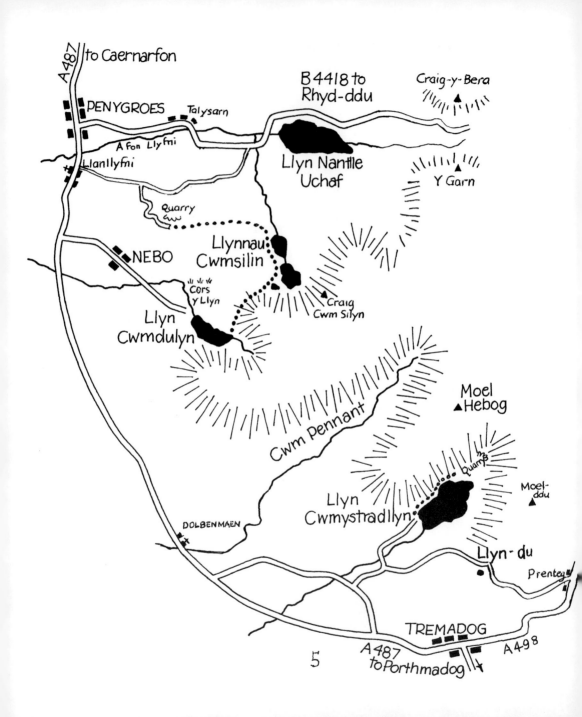

A 487
to Caernarfon

B 4418 to
Rhyd-ddu

Craig-y-Bera

PENYGROES

Talysarn

Afon Llyfni

Llanllyfni

Llyn Nantlle
Uchaf

Y Garn

Quarry

Llynnau
Cwmsilin

NEBO

Cors
y Llyn

Craig
Cwm Silyn

Llyn
Cwmdulyn

Moel
Hebog

Cwm Pennant

Quarry

Moel-
ddu

Llyn
Cwmystradllyn

DOLBENMAEN

Llyn-du

Prenteg

TREMADOG

5

A 487
to Porthmadog

A 498

Five   Cwmystradllyn and Llyn Nantlle

On the south-west flank of the Snowdonia massif are three parallel valleys lying north-east to south-west, thus following the main bias of the Caledonian folds. These valleys are all easily accessible by using the Porthmadog-Caernarfon bus service (A487).

The northernmost valley of the three has been ruthlessly exploited for slate. Going up Cwm Nantlle from Penygroes, dark purple waste tips dominate the landscape on the left with other workings on the right. Sometimes the plain little quarrymen's terraces are jewelled by the sun against the dark tips. But once beyond Talysarn, the vale of Dyffryn Nantlle begins to present a view of dramatic splendour. It is perhaps the most classical composition in the whole area, for as the crags of Craig-y-Bera and Y Garn break the skyline, they frame perfectly the peak of Yr Wyddfa in the background.

510530

No wonder that Wales's greatest painter, Richard Wilson, chose Llyn Nantlle as the foreground for his masterpiece 'Snowdon from Llyn Nantlle', at present in the Walker Art Gallery in Liverpool. By now the quarries are left behind and the view is much as Wilson saw it in the middle of the eighteenth century. It is even possible to find a similar gap in the trees at the foot of the lake to frame the foreground and with luck a couple of anglers casting their lines. Wilson's canvas is a masterpiece by any standards, yet as a topographical study it is also an accurate record, which says much for the natural beauty of the setting. It is not quite the same today, for closer study reveals that Wilson was looking across two lakes – there is a narrow band across the stretch of water which is absent now. The picture is still so similar to the present view that it is necessary to look at the first Ordnance Survey map.

The present lake is called Llyn Nantlle Uchaf (upper) implying that there must be a Llyn Nantlle Isaf (lower). Sure enough, on the old map the present lake is accurately sketched out. But there is an even bigger lake below it with only the narrowest neck of land separating them, the classic case of a large lake split in two by encroaching deltas midway. Today there is no sign of Llyn Nantlle Isaf for, as the Dorothea Quarries developed, it was found that the lakes were flooding the workings. A channel was deepened and the lower lake drained, so that what was once a large shallow lake is now water meadows. However, it makes no great difference, for the same classical view will present itself from the foot of the remaining lake.

The main valley road crosses the foot of the lake and it is one of the grandest promenades in North Wales, along this rather unprepossessing stretch of modern tarmacadam, looking up the valley along the lake through a gap at the watershed and on to the lofty bastion of Yr Wyddfa against the eastern sky.

The draining of Llyn Nantlle Isaf is significant in another way. The two Llynnau Nantlle are associated in *The Mabinogion* with the rather gruesome story of Gwydion's search for Lleu Llaw Gyffes, who after various adventures had taken the form of an eagle. In this episode, Gwydion depends on a sow as a guide.

> The swineherd opened the sty. As soon as he had opened it, she leapt forth and set off at a speed, and Gwydion followed her. And she went upstream and made for a valley which is now called Nantlleu, and there she slowed and fed. Gwydion came under the tree and looked to see what she was feeding on. And he could see the sow feeding on rotten flesh and maggots. He then looked up into the top of the tree. And when he looked he could see an eagle in the tree top. And when the eagle shook himself, the worms and the rotten flesh fell from him, and the sow eating them. And he thought that the eagle was Lleu, and sang an englyn:
>
> > *Grows an oak between two lakes,*
> > *Darkly shadowed sky and glen,*
> > *If I speak not falsely,*
> > *From Lleu's Flowers this doth come.*

With that the eagle let himself down till he was in the middle of the tree. Then Gwydion sang another englyn:

Grows an oak on upland plain
Nor rain wets it, nor heat melts;
Nine score hardships hath he suffered
In its top, Lleu Llaw Gyffes.

And he let himself down till he was on the lowest branch of the tree. And he sang this englyn then:

Grows an oak upon a steep,
The sanctuary of a fair lord;
If I speak not falsely,
Lleu will come into my lap.

And he alighted on Gwydion's knee. And then Gwydion struck him with a magic wand, so that he was in his own likeness. Yet none had ever seen on a man a more pitiful sight than was on him. He was nothing but skin and bone . . .★

All this was through the machinations of the devious Lady Blodeuedd – and retribution is finally enacted at another lake, Llyn Morwynion. But that is another story.

It is interesting, however, that the whole Leu Llaw Gyffes episode takes place 'between two lakes', confirming that even then, sometime presumably in the first millennium, there were twin lakes in Cwm Nantlle.

512508   High on the right, there is a corrie under the crags of Craig Cwm Silin. Its outflow is easily discernible as it rushes steeply down to Afon Llyfni. This long deep corrie is large enough to have the rare distinction of bearing two lakes, Llynnau Cwmsilin, at a height of 1,100 feet.

★ *The Mabinogion*, trans. by Gwyn Jones and Thomas Jones (Everyman Library, 1949)

Reaching this pair of lakes is one of the easiest and yet most rewarding walks of all. The approach is not by the steep outflow into Afon Llyfni, but further down at the opening of Cwm Nantlle. Almost opposite the old church at Llanllyfni on the main Caernarfon-Porthmadog road a lane leads up the south side of Cwm Nantlle. It twists and turns and well short of a mile there is an offshoot leading right, to the old quarry of Fronlog. It is narrow for a car, but metalled, and therefore for those not energetic enough, and insensitive enough to disturb the peace, it is an easy access to the lakes, for the lane continues safely almost all the way.

Fronlog Quarry itself is an interesting survival of pre-Industrial Revolution quarrying technology. Before the great takeover by the land barons at the start of the nineteenth century, most quarrying was conducted on a relatively small family basis, often no more than two men simply levering the slate off a small quarry face, working part-time at splitting and dressing the slates, enough only for fairly local needs. They would work a small-holding the rest of the time, according to the dictates of the season, lambing, dipping, shearing and so on. Fronlog is still worked like this today, and produces a beautiful green slate which makes not only superb rustic slates but excellent random paving.

The lane carries on past the quarry along the southern flank of Cwm Nantlle, with a grand panorama over the valley of the Dorothea Quarries (now defunct) and eventually to a view down into the water-filled pit itself, by now a deep lake in its own right. The Dorothea pit was once by repute 'the largest man-made hole in the world'. I have never been able to measure this claim against those of, say, Kimberley, etc., but it made a nice story while it lasted, and if the slate tips could be landscaped a bit and the great sheds perhaps restored to make some sort of leisure centre, it would make a fine lake facility and help restore some of the lost vigour of a once active quarry community.

On the bare slopes above Dorothea, little hamlets are clustered over the broad spine that falls away from Mynydd Mawr, an area so exposed that it says something for the hardiness of those old communities. It was on these heights that one branch of the great Irish Sea Glacier finally expended itself; many strange erratic debris, even bits of Scotland, are littered here.

The lane climbs gently and the shoulder of Cwm Silin is reached
on foot within half-an-hour. The view down into the corrie is as
fine as any. Two quite separate lakes, each roughly heart-shaped
and placed point to point, fit snugly into the cwm. Behind, the
great buttresses of Craig Cwm Silin rise precipitously to the
jagged sky-line. Looking up Cwm Nantlle the bastions of
Craig-y-Bera and Y Garn are seen from a fresh angle, with Crib y
Ddysgl (the northern flanker of Yr Wyddfa) just visible.

Below, the greenish hue of the lakes, especially of the upper one,
is most marked, pointing to copper trace elements in the rocks
above. On a sunny day, the upper lake can take on a depth of
kingfisher-blue.

The path is still clear up to the side of the lower lake and even
appears to carry on over a moraine on the near side of the lakes.
Behind this moraine is locked yet another small and shallow lake
of amazing translucence.

For the intrepid this path, by now little more than a sheep trail,
carries on steeply to the right of the Craig Cwm Silin buttresses
and provides one of the grander traverses in the area over into
Cwm Pennant.

There is one more lake in this district which is well worth a
separate walk, though by curving right and west out of Cwm
Silin over the rise, the excursion can be extended into a good half
day's walk to include Llyn Cwmdulyn. This particular shoulder
is rich in bilberry and crowberry, and on the far south-western
flanks which fall into Cwm Dulyn, where there is shelter from the
wind and full exposure to the afternoon sun, the berries are large
and early. Wheatears, stone-chats and meadow pipits are the only
company, and noticeable for their ready agitation, a sign that men
are comparatively rare visitors.

490497   But the direct approach to Llyn Cwmdulyn (and it involves only a
couple of hours on foot for the round trip) is by a narrow metalled
479505   road rising out of the little biblical village of Nebo (Nazareth is
nearby to keep the New Testament in contention and both
villages are signed clearly off the main Caernarfon-Porthmadog
road, about a mile south of Llanllyfni). The lane rises gently
towards Cwm Dulyn, with Cors y Llyn on the left, a bog of
exceedingly rich vegetation, with bog myrtle, bog asphodel, bog
cotton, spotted orchis and flags in abundance.

Cwm Dulyn is a sparse rock-strewn valley, falling down from
Bwlch Dulyn above and describing the northern boundary of
Mynydd Craig-goch. The cliffs of Craig Dulyn rise steeply above
the lake on the one side with buzzards usually soaring above
them, and green sheep slopes on the other side, falling towards
Cors y Llyn. A small dam hardly affects the long kidney-shape of
the lake, which is a reservoir. There is little vegetation in the
water, a sign of poor lime conditions. But the herring-gull have
taken possession, with their down littering both shores. It is easy
to see why – the Irish Sea is just over the way, clearly visible, with
Anglesey, Dinas Dinlle (a prehistoric battlement shaped like an
enormous ant-heap right against the shore) and Fort Belan
guarding the western end of the Menai Straits.

All the area round Cwm Silin and Cwm Dulyn is dotted with signs of human activity since prehistoric times. It might be a barely discernible hole in the ground, with a few stones littered round it, or an ancient ramp to bring down ore or quarry blocks, but most of all it is the number of abandoned small-holdings; one, called 'Fron Dulyn', with the remains of the bed still there. The old Welsh breed of cattle, the Welsh Black, still graze here, still well horned and with sleek black coats that withstand all that the weather can throw at them. Visitors might be startled after shearing time to see blue and pink sheep scattered over the slopes. The farmers seem to love covering their animals with dye.

520434 The middle valley, Cwm Pennant, is among the most favoured haunts of tourists, yet it has no lake and even the hanging valleys on its north flank, where one might expect high corrie lakes, are dry. Cwm Pennant is narrow, with natural barriers on the way up which perhaps once held back lakes. The valley's main attraction lies in the way the river has cut its way through these barriers. Strangely enough, there has been comparatively little commercial exploitation in the cwm, just a small amount of slate and copper. The main impression is of a pastoral retreat whose green valley floor is watered by the purest of streams, Afon Dwyfor.

Although it is generally assumed that the nearer a National Park aspires to 'natural' park the better, it has to be said that man's contribution has often been to its advantage. That is not a matter of Capability Brown improvement (though there are places where that too has been of great benefit in the case of fine gardens, if not parks), but rather of making the most of what deposits man has left from the past, often rendering industrial decay into something of significance in the landscape. And, of course, certain lakes have been improved by man's interference.

560444 The whole valley of Cwm Ystradllyn, the southernmost of the three valleys in the region, is such an example. Twenty-five years ago, the lake in the upper reaches of the valley was an indifferent, reedy stretch of water. Then in 1960 an earth dam raised the height of the water considerably to provide a reservoir, and I believe the larger expanse of water enhances this bare and remote valley. It is easily reached from Porthmadog (the Caernarfon-Porthmadog bus service passes the foot of the valley), but it is not as popular as its neighbour Cwm Pennant on the other side of Moel Hebog. It is a rather lonely place.

The lake lies in a large basin between Moel Hebog and Moel-ddu. Being a reservoir, it is closed to all except anglers with permits. But that is of no great moment since the lake is best viewed from the flanks on either side.

It is well worth a visit for the several man-made contributions to its environment. First, the flank of Moel Hebog on the north-west side of the lake is the site of one of the oldest and most primitive human settlements. Hut circles hug the slopes, hardly discernible amid the glacial debris and bracken.

But the great dominating feature in the valley is an old slate mill on the road up to the lake. This huge structure, with its Romanesque arched window spaces, stands like the ruins of some magnificent Burgundian abbey on a knoll in the bare rolling landscape. It was called Ynyspandy mill, built in the middle of the last century by a firm of German mining speculators. The mill was powered by the lake's outflow (the remains of the sluices are still visible), and its outworks are still more or less intact: for

Dam at Llyn Cwmystradllyn

instance, the great curving ramp on the south side where the raw slate blocks were hauled from the quarry above the lake, and the outline of the old tram-road that traverses the flanks of the hills all the way round under the Tremadog cliffs and on to the port of Porthmadog. It must have once been one of the finest buildings in North Wales and certainly it is now one of its most spectacular ruins.

Above the lake, about a mile further up at the head of the valley, is the quarry itself. Its unsightly terraces disfigure the landscape, but there is one interesting feature here too. As the quarrymen blasted their way into the mountainside, they produced an inordinate amount of waste which spilled down the hillside in such quantities that it threatened to bury the rails which provided an artery to the mill lower down. The maintenance men therefore built a high wall against this avalanche, with a corbelled overhang over the line itself. Walking under it is like passing along the lateral half of a tunnel. The size and dressing of the blocks are a monument to human endeavour – and to the false hopes of the

Ynyspandy slate mill:
Cwmystradllyn

speculators – for the quarry and its mill proved unprofitable, and they were abandoned after only a decade. This quarry is one of the last extremities of the Ordovician band and is evidence of the 'slate-rush'; although the Ordovician slates are not so viable commercially as the Cambrian – evidently the company thought it worth their while to exploit this remote valley.

As with Llyn Cwmorthin near Tan-y-Grisiau, I place Cwm Ystradllyn and its lake among my favourite walks, more because of these industrial deposits than for any intrinsic merit in the lake.

Branching off the Cwmstradllyn road to the right, about three-quarters of a mile from the main road, is a fine walk over the shoulder of Moel-ddu, which eventually falls into the Glaslyn valley at Prenteg. It takes in a small reedy lake, Llyn Du, before passing under the crags and on to Prenteg. The views west to the Clynnog Range and to the Lleyn Peninsula are an added bonus.

563425

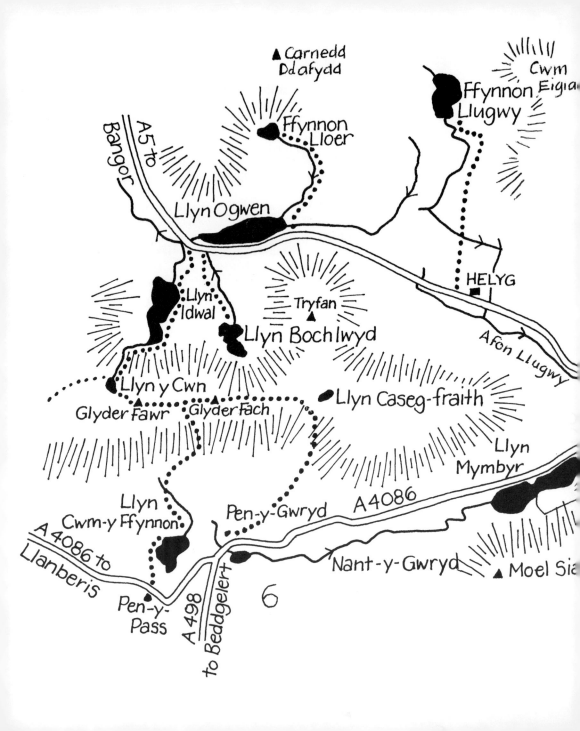

Six   Capel Curig

710575

If Yr Wyddfa is generally taken as the heart of the mountains of North Wales, Llyn Mymbyr near Capel Curig by the A4086 may be taken as the heart of its lakes. The most romantic view of Yr Wyddfa must have Llyn Mymbyr as foreground. One of the finest renderings of it is a water-colour by John Varley (1778–1842) in the Walker Art Gallery, Liverpool.

Capel Curig is an excellent touring centre. A walk along the road for about four miles west up the gently sloping Nant-y-Gwryd arrives at Pen-y-Gwryd, the old tourist inn where the earliest climbers stayed and where Everest expeditions have based their training programmes. From there Yr Wyddfa is within easy reach and Nant Gwynant lies below to the south-west. Llanberis and its lakes lie north-west over Pen-y-Pass some six miles away. Capel Curig is also within easy reach of the north-east lakes, and Llyn Cowlyd, the nearest of them, is a little over two miles away.

Llyn Mymbyr is about three-quarters of a mile long, with a delta building up midway on the north shore, practically cutting the lake in two – hence the use of the Welsh plural in some maps: 'Llynnau Mymbyr'. Nearby the Sports Council has its centre at Plas y Brenin, with courses and facilities in a whole range of activities. So Llyn Mymbyr is often covered with canoes and very pretty they look against the dark green of the conifers on the far lake shore. Llyn Mymbyr is best, though, in January when Yr Wyddfa is snow-clad, making the prospect even more picturesque.

The A5 runs through Capel Curig to the north-west, heading for more lakes. This is Telford's highroad from London to Holyhead. Before then, in Pennant's time, it was possible to pass this way only on foot or on horse-back. Pennant records that it was 'the most dreadful horse-path in Wales'.

660605

Four miles out along the A5, with the broken rock and precipices of Tryfan dominating the pass on the left, lies Llyn Ogwen, itself a centre for several fine lakes. Its ancient name is supposed to have been Ogfanw – 'young pig'. Llyn Ogwen is one of the shallowest lakes in the whole area. It averages only six feet in depth, with a maximum of only ten feet. It was probably once much deeper and its surface much higher than it is now. It is reasonable to surmise that its present outflow over Rhaeadr Ogwen was once a high rock barrier and that the outflow was formerly in the opposite direction, via Afon Llugwy towards Capel Curig. But the stream at the base of the retreating glacier cut through the rock barrier till eventually the lake began to drain at its rear over Rhaeadr Ogwen, one of the best known cascades in North Wales, and down into Nant Ffrancon. Now the watershed is half a mile back up the Capel Curig road and 60 feet above the present lake level. The outfall of streams from Llyn Bochlwyd and Ffynnon Lloer is gradually silting up the lake. From the flanks of Tryfan the subaqueous green delta of Afon Bochlwyd is readily visible under water. But it will be centuries before the beauty of Llyn Ogwen is diminished by this process.

Approaching from the Capel Curig direction (and as so often, following in the footsteps of George Borrow) the lake on a fine day becomes delicate blue, with behind it the bastions of Y Foel Goch, Mynydd Perfedd and Carnedd y Filiast. There is a public footpath across the head of Llyn Ogwen which presents the most comprehensive view of it, but the best prospect of all is from the fisherman's path on the North shore, with Tryfan rising majestically out of the waters on the far side.

Ogwen is much fished and seems always to have been. William Williams (1802) waxes eloquent on the subject:

> . . . it is well stocked with trout, which in colour and flavour surpass all fish of this kind known in any of the mountain lakes; their colour is a bright yellow; but in all other waters these fish have a darker or blackish cast externally, and when dressed are in general more white internally; but the Ogwen trout cuts as red as a salmon in full season.

He goes on to say that Ogwen has excellent eels too. According to Forrest, the sea-trout also reaches the lake and the ubiquitous minnow is there as well. But I think the angling fraternity would have been less than pleased had they seen one fisher I saw in September 1979, a shag sitting blithely on the wall by the side of the lake, patently digesting a tasty meal and ignoring the Irish juggernauts that flew past along Telford's Road, having just disembarked from the ferry. I would guess the shag's meal was more than a minnow.

Outflow from Llyn Idwal

J. M. Archer Thomson, a headmaster of Llandudno School and one of the pioneer rock-climbers in the region, quotes a strange legend from a Welsh magazine concerning Llyn Ogwen. A shepherd happened on a cave in Craig Cwrwgl above the lake containing the treasure of King Arthur. In the midst of the commotion caused by this intrusion, he turned to the lake, and 'beheld thereon a coracle in which sat three women of more than mortal beauty, but the dread aspect of the rower would have filled the stoutest heart with terror.' E. W. Steeple, who recorded this legend, suggests it 'seems a little obscure, and it may be that it has become involved with another story', probably that of Llyn Llydaw. It is not untypical of the legends of these lakes and one cannot help wondering what strange hallucinogenic aids these ancient people employed to endure the dark nights on the bare mountain.

663621 The public path across the head of Llyn Ogwen continues up the slope of Carnedd Ddafydd to Ffynnon Lloer – *parva sed apta* in its deep and almost perfect basin. At 2,000 feet above sea-level it is among the highest lakes here.

645595 Three cirque lakes in this area positively command attention. The first, Llyn Idwal, is as well known as Llyn Glaslyn and deservedly so. The path to it starts at Ogwen Cottage at the foot of Llyn Ogwen, over the stream, more a torrent over the boulders, and then turns right after a quarter-mile into the most dramatic cwm in North Wales. Llyn Idwal is surrounded by the precipitous crags of Glyder Fawr, Twll Du (the Devil's Kitchen) and Y Garn. At the head of the lake, a white *pistyll* cascades down the crags of Glyder Fawr, an almost vertical thread against the black in wet weather, yet invisible in dry spells. The acids it brings down feed the lake and account for its more than usually rich plant life.

Llyn Idwal is half a mile long, but astonishingly enough its greatest depth is only 36 feet and sixty per cent of it is under 10 feet. It is held back by a huge terminal moraine while all along the western shore are the remains of lateral moraines. The latter add a certain poetic veracity to yet another legend, that one of them is the resting place of Idwal the Giant. But William Williams suggests that the legend may be connected with Cadwaladar's son Idwal, an eighth century prince. But the legends do not end there, and remembering from its forbidding aspect that this must once

have been a secret and barely accessible place, it is no surprise. Idwal is yet another lake over which no bird is supposed to fly, though I note from personal observation that the present-day species are of an agnostic and sceptical nature. The oldest learned account of the lake's naming tells how Prince Owain Gwynedd entrusted his son Idwal to be fostered by Nefydd Hardd (Nefydd the Handsome) of Nant Conwy, who had the boy drowned in the lake. In consequence Nefydd, with all his posterity, was degraded to the rank of bondsman. There is a tradition that the land for the old church at Llanrwst was given by Nefydd Hardd in expiation for the murder.

655592 Above Llyn Ogwen and under the northern flank of Tryfan lies the second corrie lake, Llyn Bochlwyd. It is easily reached by following the stream of Afon Bochlwyd 800 feet upwards from midway along Llyn Ogwen, always skirting the boggy patches until the upper lip of the corrie is reached. Just here it is well worth negotiating the boulders to follow the stream closely where it begins to thread its way tortuously down towards Ogwen, gradually forming the delta.

Once over the lip, Llyn Bochlwyd is there, as though hardly held back by the moraine. It is quite a shallow mere, girt by morainic debris and half-filled with it. It is a beautiful sheet of water, with Tryfan rising over it to the left, grass and loose boulders at first, then sheer crags towards the summit. Ahead rise the slabs and pinnacles of Glyder Fawr and the Bristly Ridge. On the right, a col ascends to Glyder Fawr and is easily climbed for a superb view of Bochlwyd, Idwal, Ogwen and Nant Ffrancon, which latter, in the immediate post-glacial period, was also a fine long lake in all probability, with nobody around to gaze upon its beauty.

William Condry makes an interesting point about the many climbers' tents which are now pitched in summer near Llyn Bochlwyd for easy access to the climbing pitches on Tryfan. They are probably the first people to live there, he claims, since Bronze Age man.

Glacial boulders: Llyn Idwal

Before the A5's slow descent to Llyn Ogwen from Capel Curig, Afon Llugwy falls on the right, just before the watershed. About half a mile before the watershed and a quarter-mile past the cottage of Helyg, a tarmacadam road leaves the A5 at right-angles and ascends more or less directly to the cwm and the third lake, Ffynnon Llugwy. Despite being civilized by the Water Board, Ffynnon Llugwy is still one of the most interesting lakes to explore. All the way up the cwm, there is ample evidence of boulders dragged by the glacier from their moorings, and over the rise after the mile-long incline, the presence of medial moraines holding back a lake is perhaps the best example in North Wales. Ffynnon Llugwy is a reservoir and, as I say, has been somewhat civilized. Even so it remains a very fine lake and is easily accessible, though the rather military road leading up to it is deceiving, for it is in fact quite a breath-taking ascent.

688602

693625

Proceeding along the moraine on the right, there is a view of the next stage of the cwm, for Ffynnon Llugwy is in the bend of an L-shaped cwm. Straight ahead is the traverse over the shoulder of Pen-yr-Helgi to Cwm Eigiau, a splendid high walk for those not dependent on a car. Further up the cwm, the forbidding crags of Craig-yr-Ysfa provide some of the best rock climbing.

Looking back from Cwm Llugwy over the massive boulders of the moraine, Tryfan appears as an almost pure cone rising over the mirror of Llyn Ogwen.

661559

670583

Back on the Nant-y-Gwryd road (the A4086 between Capel Curig and Pen-y-Gwryd), there is a well marked path that starts at the bridge over the stream just east of Pen-y-Gwryd Hotel, up the flank of Glyder Fach in a north-east direction. It leads to the flat eastern shoulder of Glyder Fach, where it turns left and westwards over a flat moorland area towards the spectacular Castell-y-Gwynt (Castle of the Winds) and Bristly Ridge of the Glyders. On this moorland area, almost like a hole in the carpet of mat-grass, lies Llyn Caseg Fraith (perhaps the most charming name of all – 'Lake of the Dappled Mare'). On a fine autumn day this lake takes on a deep blue in the midst of the golden grass. Behind it and over Bwlch Tryfan the fortress-like aspect of Tryfan's eastern face is emphasized.

650582 The walk can now take two directions from Bwlch-y-Ddwy-Glyder midway between the two Glyders, to take in further lakes. Proceeding ahead and down the rough north flank of Glyder Fawr, the small but much celebrated Llyn-y-Cwn comes into view below, hanging over Twll-Du (The Devil's Kitchen). Its outflow falls down the 'kitchen' to feed Llyn Idwal, so that Llyn-y-Cwn properly belongs to the Ogwen system. At 2,500 feet Llyn-y-Cwn is among the highest lakes in Snowdonia and is a perfect example of so many high lakes in this mountainous area; that is, a craggy upper side and a boggy outfall, with typical attendant vegetation: the striking bogbean (found here at 2,500 feet above sea level in all the lake's exposure, and also at Llyn Tecwyn-Isaf down in the comfortable temperate 'armpit' of Tremadog Bay at only 300 feet): and the water lobelia.

637584

This long traverse, and especially Llyn-y-Cwn, is a very popular walk, but if I describe the latter as 'celebrated', how do we celebrate and propitiate the little mere's gods and fairies? We throw tin cans into it and, alas, the modern aluminium throw-away is even more durable than its predecessor.

Llyn Ogwen

From Llyn-y-Cwn the walk may take any of three directions, either to the right, down Twll-Du, to Llyn Idwal; or to the left, on a long descent to the foot of the Llanberis Pass; or back again by the Glyders and Llyn Caseg Fraith to Pen-y-Gwryd.

But there is an alternative descent from Bwlch-y-Ddwy-Glyder to Pen-y-Gwryd, which descends south from there to the bowl of Llyn Cwm-y-Ffynnon, another example of a craggy head and boggy outflow, and a lake much beloved by the anglers who visit Pen-y-Gwryd.

650563

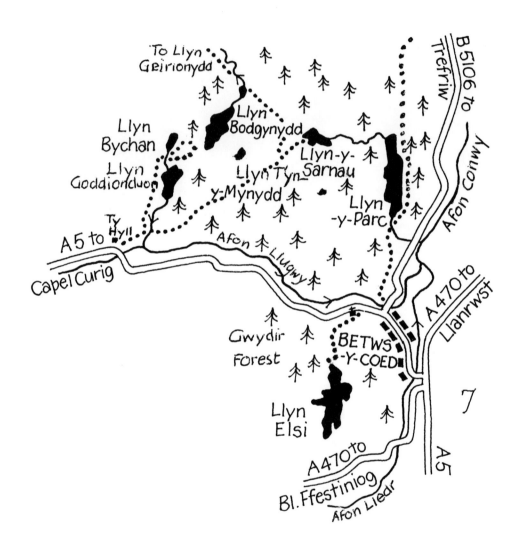

Seven   Betws-y-Coed

795565   Betws-y-Coed, snuggling in its confluence of woody glens,
seems an unlikely place for lake walkers. With rich trout and
salmon rivers like the Llugwy, the Lledr and Conwy, it is
certainly an angling centre, and as a holiday resort and staging-
post on the London-Holyhead road it has a long history.

We might complain that Betws gets a bit too popular in August,
but Bradley in 1905 was making just such a complaint, yet in the
end gave the town the benefit of the doubt for its qualities and
facilities, though he mentions no lakes.

> Bettws, there is no denying it, is not precisely the spot you
> would select in August for a quiet retreat, though it is quiet
> enough and practically unspoiled for nearly ten months of the
> year. I like to fancy it, however, as it was before the days of
> bicycles and railroads, in the early part of the century, when the
> Irish Mail dropped down here from the bleak uplands of
> Cerrig-y-Druidion and Pentre-Voelas, and prepared to face
> the wintry horrors of the Nant Ffrancon pass; when fox-
> hunting squires came hither, honeymooning in their own
> carriages, with post horses from peaceful English country
> homes in the Midlands or the East, to look with simple wonder
> at the turmoil of the mountain rivers, and see a trout rise and a
> salmon leap, for the first time most likely in their lives. How
> often, too, tucked away on the walls of back bedrooms or dark
> stairways in all parts of England does one come on souvenirs, if
> not actually of such trips, at any rate of this remote period of
> Welsh travel; quaint fly-specked woodcuts of Bettws or
> Beddgelert, with gentlemen in regency coats and high beaver
> hats, angling for salmon with implements like ships' masts,

Llyn Elsi

and ladies, decked out in the full fashion of a bygone age, posing on the bank. I like to think of Bettws, too, a little later, when David Cox and all his following of painters made the Royal Oak their headquarters, and with the anglers that foregathered there made a rare good fellowship, which went on from season to season, undisturbed by any thought of Norway salmon, or of the mountains of the moon, or by the output of bank holidays, or the rumble of the char-a-banc. But we have got to reach Bangor . . .

And we too have to see one or two lakes before moving on. But if Bradley had worries, what would he have made of our time, with a posse of Hell's Angels on motorbikes roaring up Telford's highway?

Beyond being the gateway to the mountains, there is no visible sign of a lake at Betws-y-Coed. Nor, when you learn from the map that there are indeed lakes in the neighbourhood, are they easy to find.

But among Betws-y-Coed's prides is.Llyn Elsi, which on the
1-inch Ordnance Survey map appears little more than half a mile
from the A5 as the crow flies. There is now such a labyrinth of
forest trails through endless conifers that a walker might go for
miles without finding Llyn Elsi. I confess I failed first time, and
even now seem never to come down by the way I went up. The
trail starts behind the church.

Llyn Elsi lies in a complex basin on the very top of the height
between Lledr and Llugwy valleys, a great spur with superb
views to Moel Siabod and Eryri. There are local guides on sale
which help the walker and trails are marked by spots of paint. My
own favourite (which I seem to come across rather than search
out) is marked out with mauve paint. It coincides with some
remnants of the native Gwydir forest to the north of the lake.
Vegetation is rich, especially near the old quarry, a surprising hole
in the earth to find near such an unindustrial seeming place as
Betws-y-Coed. In fact, its links with the industrial revolution are
very real, for not only was there this great quarry; to the north
there are lead mines worked from Roman times.

At any rate, once the labyrinth is mastered, Llyn Elsi is among the
most rewarding of lakes. It is unique, situated as it is on its own
height, with magnificent views all round. Its shape is complex. It
has its own little coves and several islets, one of which is covered
with bracken and birch and is therefore more colourful in winter
than in summer. The Forestry Commission have been quite
discreet about not planting right up to the shores of the lake,
though I wish they could have spared even more ground round
the lake. But the actual rocky cliffs fall into the lake and the
heather-clad banks are much as they were when Walter Crane, the
eminent *art-nouveau* illustrator, sketched it. A heron usually rises
when I arrive at the lake, and duck (the offending teal mentioned
in Carter and Lister's *Angling Notes!*). But Crane, after patently
enjoying the topography of the lake, was dissatisfied with the
ornithology and sketched a flock of eponymous cranes flying over
the water.

In 1914, Lord Ancaster allowed the people of Betws-y-Coed to take water from the lake, but beyond an inoffensive dam at its outflow, no harm has been done and a truncated obelisk commemorates the gift. Llyn Elsi is worth a lot of trouble to see in winter. Occupying as it does a hollow on an isolated height, it commands a tremendous prospect.

793584

The other significant lake in the Betws region, Llyn-y-Parc, lies on the other side of the A5, high in the forest. There is a car park just left over the old bridge at the start of the Trefriw road out of Betws. A road leads up from this car park, with the lovely Afon Llugwy threading its way over the boulders on the left. This road soon leads right and becomes a trail into the forest. The Forestry Commission has marked it as the 'Yellow Trail'. Here the timber, which reached maturity and was felled a year or two back, has given way to the most fantastic tangle of wild and possibly feral flora: predominantly acres of flaming rose-bay willow herb, orange hawkweed, St John's wort, and even a wild raspberry which yields delicious fruit in July. The whole bank is a riot of colour among the new pattern of green that must have waited under the forest floor to emerge in full daylight.

The yellow trail now takes a steeper turn up the hill at a sign saying 'Forest Trail 5 & 6', and takes on a completely different character. It ascends into a gradually narrowing ravine. Signs of old spoil heaps from the lead and zinc mines that were worked in this area and up to Llyn Geirionydd now litter the sides of the ravine. At the pinnacle of one heap near the top of the ravine (which incidentally is the outflow from Llyn-y-Parc) a self-sown pine has acquired enough toe-hold to preserve one heap from slipping eventually down the steep side of the ravine. These vertical crags, broken horizontally and vertically, with one great 'sandwich' poised on the very top waiting for the first taker, are the end of the Ordovician system which extends back as far as the Lleyn Peninsula. Over the Vale of Conwy the Silurian begins. Lower down, some of the spoil has already slipped, sending the stream underground for a space. Enormous slabs litter the bottom. It is not pretty, but highly interesting, with nature fighting to reassert itself after the abandonment of the mines in the early years of this century. Nearly 1,500 tons of lead and 700 tons of zinc were the yield from this area between 1855 and 1911. The rock and scree are a livid black with patches of white efflorescence,

Llyn Elsi

and after the wild garden below it would be somewhat forbidding if the trees, clinging to every last shelf among the beetling crags, did not redeem it.

At the top the ruins of an old mine building stand on a rough, two-stepped podium. The path levels out, with a very pastoral white cottage over a paddock on the left, then the stone and concrete dam comes into view and the prospect levels out, with forest on either side of a long blue lake, Llyn-y-Parc.

The sluice has been left open so the waters of the lake now escape to such an extent that half its bottom is exposed and has become a sort of boulder-strewn foreshore with vegetation taking over. On a hot day, a lizard will dash from a sun-warmed boulder under your feet and beyond further sight.

The west shore, comparatively sheltered from the prevailing winds, is quite reedy. Beyond that, and the dragonflies and other insects that skim over its surface, it seems a dead lake. I have not seen fish rising. Perhaps it is the effect of the mining. But it is a pretty lake none the less, stretching away between its wall of forest trees, and although Bradley's crowds in Betws itself during the high season have now reached saturation point, it is likely that after only twenty yards of the forest trail, not more than one or two walkers will be met. Which goes to show how easily deterred the mass of people are by any threat of detachment from their fellows, and what they are missing. This in turn is a blessing for those who believe a lake is worth the energy to enjoy its interest and beauty.

755575 This entire forest area in the Betws region is dotted with lakes. The best starting point for three of them is Ty Hyll (literally 'Ugly House', which is a rather handsome low cottage built of huge blocks) at the far side of the bridge halfway to Capel Curig.

753585
752592
760593
Taking the steep ascent by the right of the house, a forest trail begins on the left, which winds round and climbs to Llyn Goddionduon, hidden in trees; then Llyn Bychan on the edge of the forest, and over to the right Llyn Bodgynydd, half in and half out of the forest at its upper edge, and not far from the mines and Llyn Geirionydd (which will be taken under the Conwy system). A path from the foot of Llyn Bodgynydd leads to the Llyn Geirionydd lane and a descent back to Ty Hyll will pass the tiny mere of Llyn Ty'n-y-Mynydd on the right.

779591 An examination of the map reveals other small lakes like Llyn y Sarnau, further over in the forest past the mines, but from Betws-y-Coed, there is no doubt that the two significant lake objectives are Llyn Elsi and Llyn-y-Parc.

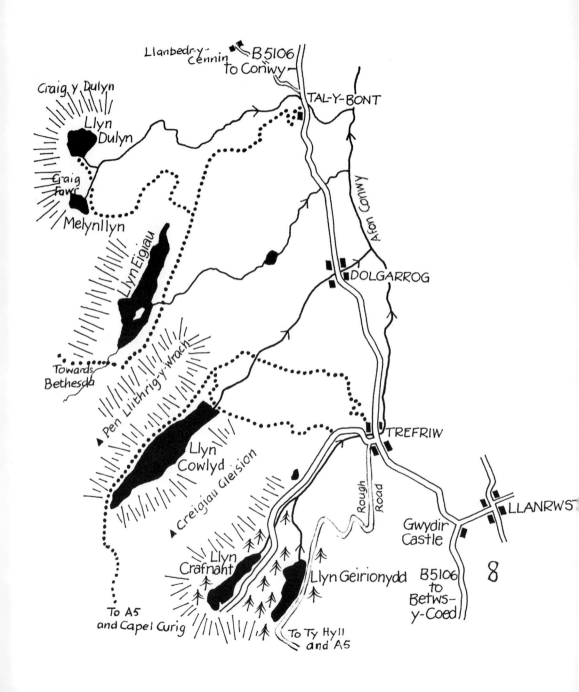

Eight Conwy

I have always found the Prologue to W. H. Auden's volume of verse *Look, Stranger* especially moving. One passage goes thus:

> *Consider the years of the measured world begun,*
> *The barren spiritual marriage of stone and water.*
> *Yet, O at this very moment of our hopeless sigh*
>
> *When inland they are thinking their thoughts but are watching these*
> *   islands,*
> *As children in Chester look to Moel Fammau to decide*
> *On picnics by the clearness or withdrawal of her treeless crown,*
>
> *Some possible dream, long coiled in the ammonite's slumber*
> *Is uncurling, prepared to lay on our talk and kindness*
> *Its military silence, its surgeons idea of pain; . . .*

It is not only the philosophical thread of the poem, when Europe was about to withdraw into the dark, but its topographical imagery that appeals to me. They are inextricably woven, of course, and Auden knew his England and Wales like the back of his hand. In this passage the view of Moel Fammau as Chester's barometer is both endearing and ominous, and it is true that from across the border Moel Fammau is the first intimation of the heights of North Wales, and of its weather. If Moel Fammau was clear and a picnic indicated, as like as not it would be in the valleys that branch off the Vale of Conwy on its west side.

From Moel Fammau westwards the hills gather height. But between the gentler hills round Moel Fammau and the austere glaciated crags of Eryri and its outliers there is that great Vale of Conwy whose flat, green bottom, from half-a-mile to one mile wide and stretching due north from Betws-y-Coed to Conwy, is most pronounced when seen from the air. It marks the boundary between two geological systems, the Silurian east of Llanrwst towards England and the Ordovician towards the mountains. It also marks the eastern boundary of the Snowdonia National Park.

Following the predominant south-west to north-east direction of the Caledonian trend, several tributary valleys flow out of the mountains on the western side of the Vale of Conwy, all containing lakes and streams flowing east and northwards, and in that respect distinct from the rest of the lakes of Snowdonia.

The four major lakes, all orientated from south-west to north-east are Geirionydd, Crafnant, Cowlyd and Eigiau.

781631   Trefriw is the best centre for all these lakes, though Llyn Cowlyd can be approached more easily from the back via Capel Curig. Trefriw was once acclaimed as a spa with its chalybeate well and as a weaving centre, using the powerful head of water from Afon Crafnant for power. I do not know whether the waters are still taken at Trefriw, but it remains both a popular holiday centre and a weaving town.

750610   The most accessible of these lakes, and therefore the most popular, is Llyn Crafnant. A steep road climbs up directly out of Trefriw, following the river which has cut a deep valley from the lake nearly three miles upstream. Llyn Crafnant (Lake of the Garlic Hollow) is rightly renowned for its beauty, with its fine profile of crags at the head of the valley. Although Crafnant is a reservoir, no disfiguring dam blocks its outflow. A simple obelisk erected by the people of Llanrwst in 1896 'commemorates the gift to that town of this lake with 19 acres of land and Cynllwyd Cottage by Richard James Esqre'.

At the upper end of the lake, as it emerges from the alluvial silt that fills the head of the cwm, the pale gold of the reeds against the black silk of the waters is a sight worth pilgrimage. There are fine walks along both shores and a full circuit is by no means strenuous and well worth the trouble for those willing to leave their cars for more than an hour. There are fine climbing pitches at the top of the valley, on the crags overlooking the lake.

Oddly enough, the next lake upstream and almost east of Crafnant, is somehow much wilder and yet not nearly so romantic in its aspect. The two lakes are separated only by Mynydd Dulyn, yet are quite different. Perhaps it is the afforestation at Geirionydd that is much less sympathetic than at Crafnant. Geirionydd lies along a fairly difficult motor traverse that rises at Ty Hyll ('The Ugly House' west of Betws-y-Coed on the Capel Curig road where the road winds over the bridge over the Afon Llugwy) and proceeds steeply up the hill until the undulating heights above the Conwy valley are reached. It is an old, dug-over area, where traces of the old lead mines are still visible amid the sterile tips. The road to the lake is signed.

It is a lake that is usually assured of a stiff breeze and sailing dinghies are moored there during the season. Picnic areas are provided along the shore and this is a bracing area, but as a whole, compared with Crafnant, the valley lacks a dramatic head, and the lake an attractive shoreline. But, as I said at the beginning, it is accessible to motorists yet is wild enough to offer that feeling of

Llyn Crafnant

apartness that is often so necessary in a world going noisily round its chosen bend. The road carries on to Trefriw or Llanrwst – it is not well signed going down and passing an oncoming car is well nigh impossible, so I would not recommend that side of the traverse. As walking country, however, this partially industrial wasteland is interesting enough, and in any case, the walker will always see far more than any motorist. But I still find it hard to say why I find Crafnant so romantic and Geirionydd so wild, but workaday.

I think I must this once come down hard on the foresters, whose picnic areas and parking areas are well intentioned, but whose actual tree-planting in this case is harsh of line, colour and shape. However, Geirionydd has one claim of a romantic nature – it was traditionally the home of the sixth-century Welsh Bard, Taliesin.

769631
716591
Back at the centre of Trefriw, it is possible to approach the third Conwy lake, Llyn Cowlyd, by a fork right off the Crafnant road, but it is best approached from the rear, as I have pointed out in the Capel Curig section. It is an easy walk across the gently rising grassland, starting from Tal-y-Waen about one mile out from Capel Curig on the Ogwen road. It can be very wet so strong waterproof gear is recommended. The path is quite straightforward and is both marked and marred by the remains of an old telephone or electric cable. There has been a half-hearted attempt to fell the poles, none whatsoever to clear the smashed insulators whose highly glazed ceramic is of course imperishable. Government departments and semi-state bodies are occasionally among the worst despoilers of our landscape and this old battlefield of electric wires is one among several eyesores in North Wales that could be attributed to such intervention.

720613
The path, then, aims for the gap between Pen Llithrig-y-Wrach (Slippery Witch's Head) on the left and Creigiau Gliesion on the right. At the watershed, man-made leets crossed by solid bridges indicate the proximity of a reservoir, and shortly after crossing one the path descends sharply with Llyn Cowlyd ahead. From this angle, it seems an extraordinarily light lake. Its surface reflects the sky with nothing to close off the light at the end, where a dam holds it above the long descent into Nant Conwy at Dolgarrog, a town which in the 'twenties suffered the most appalling inundation with considerable loss of life, from a dam breaking above during a storm.

Llyn Cowlyd is the largest of the Conwy lakes. The slopes all round fall into the water steeply, so are not likely to encourage foresters. The consequent bareness gives Cowlyd a character all its own, not a tree in sight and little bird life.

But it was not always so, if we are to believe *The Mabinogion*. The most convoluted story in that collection of old tales is 'Culhwch and Olwen', in which Culhwch, to win Olwen as his bride, must perform almost impossible labours for her father, the giant Ysbaddaden. Culhwch recruits his first cousin King Arthur to set about the innumerable tasks.

At one stage a succession of mythical beasts are consulted on the whereabouts of Mabon, son of Modron, the freeing of whom from dreadful imprisonment is one of Culhwch's labours. Among the creatures is the Owl of Cwm Cowlyd:

> They came to a place where the Owl of Cwm Cawlwyd was. 'Owl of Cwm Cawlwyd, here are Arthur's messengers. Knowest thou aught of Mabon son of Modron, who was taken away from his mother when three nights old?' 'If I knew it, I would tell it. When first I came hither, the great valley you see was a wooded glen, and a race of men came thereto and it was laid waste. And the second wood grew therein, and this wood is the third. And as for me, why! the roots of my wings are mere stumps. From that day to this I have heard naught of the man you are asking after. Nevertheless I will be guide to Arthur's messengers until you come to the place where is the oldest creature that is in the world, and he that has fared farthest afield, the Eagle of Gwernabwy.

If this is to be given any sort of credence, it confirms that the valley was once wooded, as most of Snowdonia, but that the first denudation took place much earlier than mediaeval times, which is more unusual. It is known that the earliest prehistoric settlers cleared some of the area and perhaps the story remembers this first felling, then the natural regeneration, the second felling and a second regeneration.

And there is added mystery, too, in its depth, for Llyn Cowlyd is the deepest lake in North Wales at 222 feet. Those steep flanks continue down into the lake for some time as can well be imagined when looking at the lake from either end.

But of all the Conwy lakes, the northern-most trio, Llyn Eigiau, with its neighbours Melynllyn and Llyn Dulyn, offers the greatest adventure, for not only does the approach open up a wide stretch of very interesting landscape, but at the head of the great wide cwm there are corries that exemplify more than any the meaning of that word.

The approach is long – a full day's walk. For motorists, only those willing to keep down to first gear and to reverse up a one-in-four gradient to allow an ascending vehicle to pass will wish to tackle 767688 it. At the village of Tal-y-bont, about a mile north of Dolgarrog on the west side of Nant Conwy, there are two minor roads branching off left. The first, unsigned, is the Cwm Eigiau approach and may be unmarked because by no means can it be counted as a motor road. The second, marked 'Llanbedr-y-cennin' is to be avoided – it does not go to Cwm Eigiau.

So, take the first road up from Tal-y-bont, it winds steeply up, just as with the Crafnant and Geirionydd approaches, for well over a mile before it flattens out into the broad cwm of Eigiau. Do not take the tempting left fork at the top of the ascent. This is wild, wind-swept land, exposed to the north, so not advisable for winter excursions. There is only the absolute minimum of settlement in Cwm Eigiau, yet the area has seen man's continuous presence since prehistoric times, as witnessed by the occasional tumuli or hut-circles (Ardda Village on the lower slopes of Moel Eilio, marked on the O.S. map) and the old mediaeval church of Llangelynin perched not far away, high above Nant Conwy.

735663 After this winding ascent, the road straightens out across the boggy opening towards Cwm Eigiau, which lies in front with the hump of Pen Llithrig-y-Wrach rising at its head. The road seems to lead nowhere and even the name Trasbwll marked on the O.S. map is little more than a ruin in the middle of the bog.

But here is a choice of direction; there is a sign marked 'No Parking – Turning Point for Farmer'. He is quite right – a carelessly parked tourist car could hold him up in his sheep round while some happy walker is breathing in the sweet air a thousand feet up somewhere.

Ahead lies Llyn Eigiau, and certainly the road continues straight to its outlet, but it is increasingly boggy ground and the path can often become a stream.

720650 Llyn Eigiau is a strange lake, one-sided and somehow just not spilling out on its open side. On the west side of the lake, crags fall precipitously into the lake, while on its long eastern shore there seems nothing to hold back a lake, only bogland, and that now has a long retaining wall, a marvel of building in its way. Llyn Eigiau is a reservoir. If that bogland slipped, the lake would simply drain off into the peat and become little more than a small tarn; its present mean depth is only nine feet.

Cwm Eigiau continues up beyond the head of the lake, winding eventually up to the heights and over to either Bethesda or the north coast. This is one of the grand high traverses of Snowdonia, passing under the brow of Carnedd Llewelyn.

732663   At the 'No Parking' sign, a well defined path leads firmly right, through a gate, up on to and round the shoulder, where you can view Llyn Eigiau, then after quite a long haul into two of the most dramatic corries in Snowdonia.

702658   The crags that form these two distinctive corries warrant their own definitive names. The first, holding Melynllyn, is called Craig-fawr, and the second Craig y Dulyn. A strange lateral moraine, huge boulders sticking out of its grassy hump, holds in Melynllyn, and is so even that it might have been formed by some giant bulldozer. It forces the outflow right and there a dam was built (now in a state of some disrepair) – for all three lakes, Eigiau, Melynllyn and Dulyn have been exploited as reservoirs.

700665   It is a short, slight ascent, then a steep descent to Llyn Dulyn, hidden behind a shoulder and surely the most dramatic rock-basin anywhere. The mean depth of the lake is 104 feet, its maximum 189, which for a lake less than a quarter-mile long is astonishing.

At its top side, Craig y Dulyn falls so steeply into the waters that only three feet from the shore a depth of 55 feet was recorded by Mr Jehu. I imagine him in 1900, still the great age of Victorian exploration, his punt carried up the long ascent by native Welsh bearers, and his gratification at plumbing that immense depth only three feet from the wall of vertical rock. It proved his thesis, that these corrie lakes were indeed rock-basins, previously a matter of speculation only, based more upon observation of the Swiss lakes than the Welsh ones.

Although, like its neighbours Melynllyn and Eigiau, Llyn Dulyn has been altered by the water-engineers (it supplies Llandudno), it is nevertheless an exciting phenomenon. That vast hole is only too apparent, the sheer black depth of the lake is as obvious as Eigiau's shallowness. All three lakes bear the tell-tale tidemark of reservoirs, but in Dulyn's case, despite quite elaborate works round the dam, it seems to matter least. The rock at its head is so perpendicular that only a very few mosses and lichens seem to survive there. But to the left, the north-east face of the basin, although still steep and broken with rock debris, is rich in flora, especially ferns, and alpine botanists would surely find the corrie rewarding, for at 1,747 feet above sea level, it must be one of the coolest in the country. One strange phenomenon I noticed in early September was the tiny orange-coloured fungus that peeps like a polished berry out of the thick mat of heather and bilberry.

The lonely and austere situation and aspect of Llyn Dulyn is such a contrast to arboreal Llyn Mair near Maentwrog in the Blaenau Ffestiniog system, that it is a measure of the range of the lakes of Snowdonia. I would place the entire Llyn Dulyn excursion among the most exciting walks in Snowdonia.

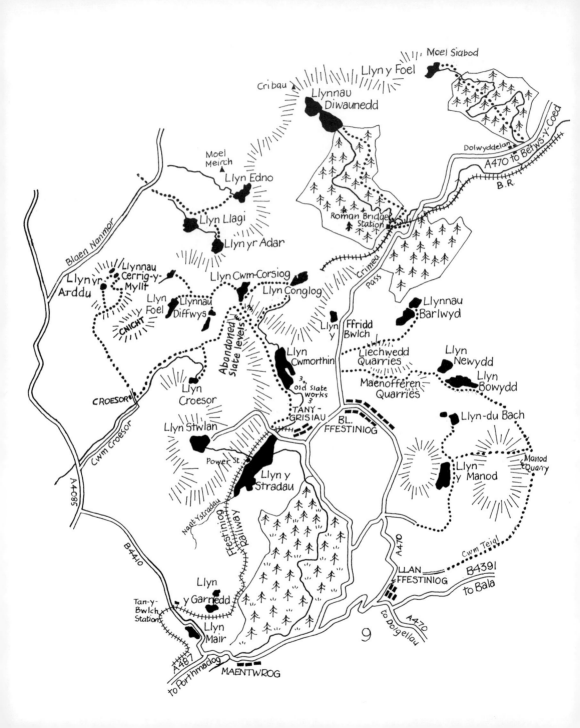

Nine   Blaenau Ffestiniog

When Parc Genedlaethol Eryri (Snowdonia National Park) was designated in 1952 the quarry area of Blaenau Ffestiniog was studiously excluded, a small devastated enclave locked in by natural beauty all round. In a way it was a sort of snub to Blaenau, a chastisement for getting itself into such a mess. That was the view then, when both Blaenau Ffestiniog and its near neighbour Tanygrisiau were neglected as tourist centres and the general air of decay, slate tips, contracting quarries and consequent unemployment made a sort of black spot surrounded by green National Park.

Blaenau is still excluded from the Park, a besieged area really, and local unemployment is a greater problem than ever. To be fair, the exclusion from the National Park was fully intended to attract alternative industries and development otherwise prohibited or discouraged in the Parks.

The subsequent development of the old slate-mines as tourist attractions, along with the Tanygrisiau pump-storage scheme, has at last brought new life in summer during the tourist season. By now, from being a place to drive through as quickly as possible (though personally I never thought of Blaenau in such terms, having a great affection for it), it is one of the most popular centres in North Wales. In a generation, taste and values have changed to such an extent that Blaenau can live in hope again. As a subject, industrial archaeology was in its infancy when the Parks were being designated; now it is a business. In Blaenau Ffestiniog it has become big business, as we shall see, and no place deserves success more. But it is still only seasonal success, and in a few cases it is not without its indignities. The quarry craftsman has

become a tourist guide showing off his former life and work-style as a sort of remote history.

People are not easily convinced that Blaenau, off-season, has its attractions, provided the weather is right. It rains over one hundred days each year. Yet a fine October weekend in Blaenau is a pleasure to be compared with anything we have in the way of walking in these islands.

The region, as far as the lakes are concerned, is both compact and complex. The main outflow for the hills immediately around Blaenau itself is to the south, via the Afon Dwyryd and the Vale of Ffestiniog to Traeth Bach on Tremadog Bay, and many small lakes around Blaenau and its associated village of Tanygrisiau flow into this system.

But not very far off in 'crow miles', over the many ridges and shoulders that enclose Blaenau in a vast amphitheatre, there are more lakes, finding their way into other systems, like those in the valley west of Blaenau, Blaen Nanmor, which ultimately join the Glaslyn system, or others, to the east, over the Crimea Pass (the A470 to Betws-y-Coed) which join the Conwy system.

679460

For the Dwyryd system, Tanygrisiau, the little slate village one mile west of Blaenau Ffestiniog is an excellent base, not very far from the main lake in the system, Llyn Cwmorthin, which is reached by ascending the ramp of the abandoned quarry tramway that rises at the base of the spoil heaps north-west of the village. The ascent up this ramp is extraordinary. Built of slate rubble, it climbs at the side of Llyn Cwmorthin's outflow, an extremely lively little river twisting and turning between boulders and falling over shelves of rock, with one spectacular water-slide. Higher up, the river has been harnessed between elaborately built slate walls to work the machinery that sawed and planed the slate. The mountain flanks on either side, where they are not covered with slate waste, rise in smooth hummocks – a sign of the slate below – alternating with angular granite blocks, occasionally detached by the glacier and left stranded. The predominant grey is broken by areas of red oxide, with the crystal clear waters threading their way over and through them. In summer, the local children love to splash, paddle and swim in the pools under the water-slides.

Below Llyn Cwmorthin

On the ramp, the climb keeps to a steady angle, then levels out to an extensive area of abandoned slate sheds. All round rise walls of slate, strangely reminiscent of Inca building. There is a similar remoteness up in the hills, an apartness, the same sheer surfaces of tightly-knit stone fabric, surrounded by smooth, sheep-bitten grass slopes. The great difference, of course, lies in the size of the blocks.

And there ahead, shimmering in the sun amid this half-devastated landscape, is the lake with its outflow lapping over a low man-made sill.

Llyn Cwmorthin may not be the prettiest lake, but I do find it one of the most interesting. It lies in the classic type of glaciated valley with a rock barrier at its foot holding back a bow-shaped lake about a third of a mile long. Llyn Cwmorthin is a good base for smaller lakes further up in the same system.

Like so much of the neighbourhood, the valley has been extensively worked over for slate, then abandoned, or rather – and this I find touching – almost, but not quite. A solitary slate worker still splits a few blocks, turning out damp-proof course, small roofing slates and paving slabs – a sort of last cowboy in the West! The whole valley has a look of the Klondike, worked out for wealth then left derelict. Yet there is so much to see, especially in the way of lakes. There is everything from the remotest upland lake, rarely visited by people, poised like Llyn Conglog at 2,000 feet in a high basin, to a busy man-made reservoir like Llyn-y-Stradau, fished by 20,000 anglers each year.

Llyn Cwmorthin is about a quarter of a mile below the head of the valley, an example of alluvial silting. The path takes the left, south-western shore and was once a very important avenue for traffic. First the drovers used it, coming from Cwm Croesor and beyond, then the quarry workers. A ruined chapel half-way along, as though decently removed from the material concerns of life at the head and foot of the valley, answered the spiritual needs of the quarrymen, for they were staunchly religious, as the minutes of their *caban* (a sort of debating society) reveal. Now only cattle and sheep haunt the chapel's damp precincts. The walls bear fantastic efflorescent murals of especial interest to connoisseurs of the *tachiste* school of painting.

Outflow: Cwmorthin

Llyn Cwmorthin is distinctly a dry weather excursion. I have seen the cwm filled with rain, the stream milk-white with spume, and visibility down to ten yards. Yet I love Cwmorthin as much as any of the lakes and my enthusiasm was shared by Pennant. But he saw it before the desolation of the slate tips, when it must have been green and pristine.

665463 At the head of the valley, another half-ramp half-path climbs steeply up to the level head of the pass over to Cwm Croesor, and here again slate works must once have echoed with the sounds of drilling, sawing and splitting slate. Now the prevailing sounds come from sheep, curlews and ravens. Choughs sail in the wind overhead and scold visitors.

This is a bleak area, a corridor for the prevailing sou'-westers. Water abounds, and there are lakes all round, each hidden in its secret hollow. Only in fine weather should they be explored, for on many a day cloud comes up from Cwm Croesor and the whole area becomes treacherous with numerous false directions inviting the unwary walker over yet more inhospitable bogs and rock faces.

663470 However, given that the weather is fine and that there have been no rains to speak of for some time, the country to the right above the quarry-works is very interesting. Despite the height (the watershed itself is 1,427 feet above sea level) Llyn Cwm-Corsiog at nearly 1,800 feet was once held back by a fine dam, divided into two sections by a rocky hump, which seems to have anchored the dam. Pipes, remnants of rails, iron stanchions and so on all the way down to the works are witness to the lengths (and heights) those nineteenth-century gentlemen would go to extract and work their slate. Evidently they needed large quantities of water (all the great saw blades had to be cooled by water as they cut through the slate blocks). Anything that could be dammed was carefully shored up, and lower down, nearer the works, remains even the debris of a wooden dam across the stream from Llyn Cwm-Corsiog.

All this meant considerable investment, even with low labour costs, but slate was a wealthy commodity. It really roofed the world in the last century as row after row of terraces went up to house the increasing number of urban workers. Slate quarried, sawn, split and dressed into roofing slates on this bleak plateau area of the watershed would descend the great Rhosydd Quarry ramp into Cwm Croesor, thence by tramway to Porthmadog where it was shipped by sailing craft to all corners of the earth. All this is now but industrial archaeology. We are intrigued and fascinated by it and in some cases, as with the Festiniog Railway or the Llechwedd Quarry at Blaenau Ffestiniog, we even resuscitate it as a tourist attraction, but none of us would exchange for the life of a quarryman working his heart out on that bleak watershed for wages that barely kept a family. Not until recently was it recognized that men who had succumbed to the dread disease of silicosis deserved some form of compensation.

Llyn Cwm-Corsiog

Llyn Cwm-Corsiog is a wild and silent place, whose two or three boulders, strewn like dice in its waters, provide a favourite perch for the gulls. There is only the most vestigial track, more a sheep path, and the best direction is to climb due north by compass from the slate-works. Another indicator of the lake's existence is the fact that the stream that feeds the ruined slate mill at the end of the watershed is the outflow from Llyn Cwm-Corsiog.

659468 Continuing from Llyn Cwm-Corsiog, by curving round west-ward then and towards the shoulder of Cnicht (the finest view of which is from hereabouts) the Llynnau Diffwys come into view below. They hang over the steep valley head of Cwm Croesor, hence the name 'Precipice Lakes'. Hanging over Cwm Croesor as they do they have an end-of-the-world air, and the only sign of life I saw there recently was a pair of sand-pipers – but these delightfully sharp little waders are enough to bestow life on any wilderness.

655468 Due west of Llynnau Diffwys, right under the steep shoulder of Cnicht, lies Llyn Cwm-y-Foel. It is a reservoir and its waters once turned the turbines in the power-house at the head of Cwm Croesor's valley floor. Not long after World War II, its dam showed signs of cracking and needed urgent repair if the village of Croesor was not to be flooded. The problem was how to get heavy loads of cement and aggregate up there (it seemed to present no problem in the previous century, judging by the numerous works on so many of these upper lakes). Mules were considered – where to get such beasts these days? – then abandoned in favour of a helicopter. It is a sign of the aerial turbulence at the heads of these valleys that the helicopter crashed, fortunately with only minor injuries to the pilot. I can remember the baleful headline in a Welsh weekly at a time when there was perhaps less pride in the language than there is now: 'Mae Helicopter yn Crashio!'

674474 But if the way is to be eastward from Llyn Cwm-Corsiog rather than westward (it never does to be too ambitious on these heights and one direction at a time is advisable), a fairly steep climb nearly 600 feet takes you to the largest of these upper lakes – Llyn Conglog at 2,000 feet above sea level. Its outflow (it would be called a 'ghyll' in Cumbria, but here it is a 'pistyll') falls over the steep glaciated side of Cwmorthin and joins the river just above the lake, thus contributing considerably to the alluvial silting of Llyn Cwmorthin.

But for the really fit and athletic walker, I strongly recommend the Llyn Conglog excursion by this *pistyll* directly up out of Cwmorthin. The *pistyll* is in fact the source of Llyn Cwmorthin and falls just where the cwm bends, about a quarter-mile above the head of the lake. Looking up the *pistyll* at this point, it looks a pretty daunting climb, but it is well worth the trouble. After nearly a thousand feet of scrambling over grass, bed rock and block scree either side of the plunging stream, the going suddenly gets easier through a sort of little gorge which the stream has cut over the shoulder of the valley.

From below there is no sign of this, of course, so it is rather a surprise, a pleasant one after the hard going up the valley side. After no more than seven or eight minutes, Llyn Conglog comes into view. This is surely the proper dramatic approach to the fine upland lake. It is wild, wind-swept, with no vegetation but sheep grass all round. The lake has a long peninsula, with the underlying rock exposed at the water's edge.

Llyn-y-Foel

This entire wild area, with its numerous little tarns, is very inviting territory to tramp over. A circuit along the right of the lake brings into view the Crimea Pass, with a glimpse of Llyn Iwerddon poised in a little hollow between the crags that overhang the pass, and Moel Siabod on the skyline. But to get back to Cwmorthin (assuming it be necessary to return to base) it is necessary to keep circling Llyn Conglog to the neck of the peninsula and then, once the low brow ahead is negotiated, to get into line with Llyn Cwm-Corsiog, visible below, with Llynnau Diffwys further over.

The rest is merely a matter of avoiding the worst areas of sphagnum to return to the head of Cwmorthin and the slate works. Starting from Tanygrisiau, this is a strenuous walk and takes more than an afternoon. But the incidental rewards are many, not least the fact that in high summer, that difficult ascent up the *pistyll* keeps your nose to the ground and it seems to me one of the loveliest bits of ground in all North Wales, for beneath the tufts of grass, the most beautiful wild flowers vie in colour for your attention, with tiny milkwort shining with the purest gentian blue imaginable.

680440 Conveniently associated with Llyn Cwmorthin by now, and in terms of popularity even eclipsing it, are two new lakes. Or at any rate, one new one and one enlarged corrie lake: Llyn-y-Stradau (or Tanygrisiau Reservoir as the Ordnance Survey gracelessly but more accurately describes it) and Llyn Stwlan respectively. Tanygrisiau once again is the base.

Both lakes owe their present existence to developments by the Central Electricity Generating Board in the 'sixties, and that body's design and environment experts have made a good job of what might have been a hideous exploitation of one of North Wales' finest pair of peaks, the Moelwyns.

One of the problems of an atomic power station like Trawsfynydd, just four miles away across the Vale of Maentwrog, is that the tremendous heat generated by nuclear fission cannot be damped down during off-peak periods as it can in fossil-fuelled stations. It simply goes on producing its maximum of heat, and naturally engineers exercised their ingenuity to use up this surplus during off-peak periods. Two lakes in tandem, one above the other, provide the answer. Pump water up from the lower to the higher with the atomic off-peak surplus, then during peak demand, release the water back down through a normal water turbine to boost the grid. As I have said in the Llanberis chapter, this involves a moral choice, environment versus national power requirements.

The Tanygrisiau scheme is a good example, therefore, to judge the results. To take the lower lake first, Llyn-y-Stradau. This occupies, just below the village of Tanygrisiau, what was once a swampy valley where the old narrow-gauge Festiniog Railway began its descent to Porthmadog with its burden of industrial slates. The end of the valley was dammed and the resulting lake gradually filled, drowning what was left of the railway line.

At the time of its planning, there were only paper plans to resuscitate the Festiniog Railway, now world famous as one of the country's most magnificent narrow-gauge lines. After years of desuetude, enthusiasts were quick off the mark and the redevelopment of the line began to take place at about the same time as work began on the dam of Llyn-y-Stradau. So the first anomaly posed by the new lake was the loss of the upper end of the railway, which cut the fun by half.

In fact, railway enthusiasm knows no bounds. A country run by such people would have neither management nor labour problems. By the ingenious introduction of a loop to gain height just before the lake, the railway was raised to a higher contour, enabling it to circumvent the lake and thus to complete its journey to Tanygrisiau. (The extra mile that will bring the line up to Blaenau Ffestiniog BR terminal is a simple matter compared with the work of passing the lake and will only be a matter of time.) But the conjunction of the resuscitated railway with the new lake has created one of the most popular amenities in North Wales.

Llyn-y-Stradau is nearly a mile long, and as far as looks go, it works, being a great deal better to behold than the former boggy stretch. There are splendid walks all round it and up into the Moelwyns. The power station itself sits low in the landscape and is well designed with granite walling. Most of all, however, it is an anglers' lake. The CEGB has made the most of this, stocking the lake from its Fish Farm at Trawsfynydd. They organize competitions and control catches. As a measure of its popularity, 19,343 anglers fished there in 1979, catching 21,374 trout from 27,157 stocked, and the heaviest single fish weighed 10 pounds 4 ounces. The overall record fish from the lake has been 12 pounds, which is some trout by any standards!

For the non-angling fraternity like myself, it is fascinating to dip just a little into the arcane list of flies and lures recommended for catching these delectable trout. In 'early season', a 'Bloody Butcher' (this shakes my faith in anglers), a 'Mallard and Claret' (this restores it) and 'Zulu' are recommended, while in 'July–September' there is a 'Missionary' and 'Soldier Palmer', while for September and October, a 'Connemara Black' and 'Baby Doll' are the very thing. Obviously, I am missing something. But I confess I would not enjoy sharing it with twenty thousand others, and if I did fish, I have no doubt I would end up at some barely accessible upland tarn, landing perhaps three four-ounce trout per season and confining the 'Mallard and Claret' to the refreshments.

Looking at the lake from Tanygrisiau, the stream that feeds it, Nant-y-Stradau, enters at the far end, with a tributary, Afon Stwlan, just this side of the power station, which is the outflow from the corrie high above, locked between Moelwyn Mawr and Moelwyn Bach.

665445 Llyn Stwlan (on the first Ordnance Survey map of 1838 it is named 'Llyn Trawstyllon') was formerly a small corrie lake. The dam sits on the mountainside and is visible for miles from the Trawsfynydd direction. It is now easily accessible by the new road which climbs the flank of the mountain. In summer a bus travels at regular intervals.

For further lake walks in this region it is necessary to take as starting point the two valleys west of Blaenau Ffestiniog which both lead up from the A4085 between Penrhyndeudraeth and Aberglaslyn.

630448 The first, Cwm Croesor, is of course the other side of the Cwmorthin watershed, so all the lakes accessible from the latter can be equally well reached from Cwm Croesor, and a road leads up the valley from the A4085 to the village of Croesor itself. From there, an hour's walk to the head of the valley is sufficient to reach

Yr Arddu

the watershed with Llynnau Diffwys first and the others following.

But Croesor is also the centre for three very individual lakes lying
high in basins on the knobbly heights of Yr Arddu nearly two
miles north of the village. The lumpy volcanic forms of Yr Arddu
are worth exploring on their own. From the O.S. map this might
look easier than it is in fact, but a path does lead up west from the
village of Croesor, following at first the old drovers' road that
rises out of the village left of the chapel, and then branching off
right at the crest, up towards Yr Arddu and Cnicht. This is the
recognized route up Cnicht, but about half-a-mile out into the
humpy pasture, the further turn right indicated for Cnicht by a
post should be ignored. Yr Arddu is roughly ahead and left of the
obvious pass called Bwlch-y-Battel. So head for this pass. The
outlying ridges of Yr Arddu circle east and north. The hoary
knobs and ridges of granite fall away towards Nantmor in
spectacular fashion, split over centuries of weathering into
enormous smooth-topped loaf-shapes.

637465

It is within this circle of crags that Llyn yr Arddu is enshrined, a beautiful little lake in its especial basin. There can be a sublime silence within this basin high up on the knobs of Yr Arddu, a silence broken only by the ripple of water against granite slab. The wonder of waters like Llyn yr Arddu, isolated on a detached height, is that however serious the drought (as in '59, '76 or the spring of '80) the level never seems to drop, which goes to show how water is secreted in the ground in even the highest basins. The granite of the basin is impervious, of course, so that the only loss after the outflow is by evaporation.

628466

The pair of lakes called Llynnau Cerrig-y-Myllt are a good half-a-mile further north-east and the going from Llyn yr Arddu is very rough indeed. The best approach is from the top of Bwlch-y-Battel itself. Once again, after a rise over the crags, the basin lies just over the rim. Two lakes in tandem are always a fine sight and these two, high up in their own isolated eyrie, are among the wildest. One is higher than the other, and the one does not flow into the other – they have separate outflows into the same hanging valley above Nantmor. Contrary to what I have noticed elsewhere, the lower lake can lose its level in a drought, and in the spring of '80, with drying winds all the time and Snowdonia ravaged by huge forest fires, this was all too apparent – a loss of one foot was clearly visible by the 'tide-mark', and the outflow quite dry. Oddly enough, the two shore lines seem to differ in colour, the upper one a bleached white, the lower one more an oxide red – probably due to its liability to lose height during droughts. The upper one boasts a grassy islet, on which black-capped gulls like to rest and preen themselves when not dipping and soaring in the turbulence above the basin.

632472

The next valley west, Blaen Nanmor, brings fresh lakes within reach. Once again a road leads up from the A4085. Nanmor, like the Cwmorthin/Cwm Croesor watershed, is scarred by quarry workings. Among the works is a public path signed on both sides of the road. Starting eastwards from this point, keep to the left of both white houses and the rest is cairned.

607447

635490

Following the cascades on the way, the path levels out and the going can often be very wet. The first lake is soon apparent. It is a corrie lake and its outlet struggles over the lip above the cascades. Llyn Llagi itself is austere and beautiful, with an imposing dark wall behind it. Once, as we came up to it, a heron sailed a foot over the lake's surface for our very private delectation. There are fine views of Snowdon and Llyn Dinas.

649482

The main footpath continues up the flank to the left of the lake, and after a steady climb round a col on the right, Llyn-yr-Adar comes into view.

655482

It lies on a rough plateau where the ridge of Cnicht flattens out. The place is a bleak brown colour most of the year, so one can understand why Adar is best known for its emerald islet, which manages to stay a bright green all the year round and thus to provide relief for the eye. The lake flows out by a flat clear stream which then tumbles down over the lip in a straight line to Llagi.

Llynnau Cerrig-y-Myllt

The path veers left on the way up past Llyn Llagi, to avoid the precipitous slopes of its corrie, then proceeds right up the shoulder to Llyn-yr-Adar. But if, instead of climbing to the right, you keep straight ahead for the flat top of the obvious pass above, one of the best lakes in Snowdonia will be your reward for a stiff climb. On the way, high on the left above the path, is an outcrop of quartz, with white debris falling away from it across the path, and even being employed as building material for an old sheep-pen. Of course, in a volcanic area like Snowdonia, such evidence of quartz is not uncommon (there is an outcrop near the top of Cwm Nantlle and another on the Ffestiniog side of the Crimea Pass), but this one is particularly hoary in its aspect.

Looking back across the face of the Llyn Llagi corrie, there is the height of Yr Arddu two miles away, and what looks like one of those lakes that are captured in the craters of extinct volcanoes, because it lies in a high hollow on its own isolated eminence, with crags falling away from it all round. It is in fact two lakes, Llynnau Cerrig-y-Myllt, with a third sheet of water, out of sight, right under the crags of Yr Arddu itself, Llyn yr Arddu, all of which we have dealt with on page 130.

But to continue the walk up to the water-shed, which is a typical rock-strewn wilderness of fescue grass, with only the indifferent sheep and the carrion crows for company, hollows fall away on all sides, except for the shoulder up towards Cnicht and Llyn-yr-Adar. A careful reading of the O.S. map is advisable, for although there is no marked path here, certain peaks from Moel Hebog to the Glyders may be pin-pointed. The views of Yr Wyddfa on the way up are probably the best in the whole area, with the great divide of Nant Gwynant lying between to distance the whole massif. At the very top, where on a windy day you can hardly stand, the view east is dramatic, with Moel Siabod just over the way and the land falling away towards England over the far horizon.

662498 In one of the hollows on this windswept height at about 1,800 feet above sea level lies Llyn Edno, austere, crystalline in its hollow, with granite slabs falling into its eastern shore. Looking back, its rock barrier is all too apparent, with a gap neatly worn into the dip of the geological fold for its outflow. Out of the wind in the sheltered hollow of Llyn Edno, the contrasting silence is broken only by the rise of a trout.

To walk just north of the lake, to Moel Meirch, at just short of 2,000 feet, is well worth the extra effort, providing the finest belvedere of all for a view towards Yr Wyddfa and its outliers to the north-west.

South of Blaenau Ffestiniog, there is one detached roadside lake, which might be discussed here for convenience; it does not fit into a ready walking excursion along with other lakes. Yet it is far from negligible, for it has its own serene tree-girt beauty and contrasts sharply with the more austere upland lakes.

653412 Llyn Mair lies only half a mile uphill from the Oakley Arms, near Maentwrog, on the Llanfrothen road (B4410) (which incidentally is a perfectly good alternative to crossing Traeth Mawr by the Porthmadog tollgate). Because it is by the roadside, Llyn Mair, like Llyn Dinas, is a popular lake, yet it is never crowded. Actually it is the last lake in its own little system, for from its source on the southern flank of Moelwyn Bach, its stream passes through first Llyn y Garnedd Uchaf (the upper) in the middle of the forestry above Tan-y-Bwlch station on the Festiniog Railway (a good starting-point for Llyn Mair), then through Llyn y Garnedd Isaf (the lower), before passing into Llyn Mair.

Naturally, since tourists visit the lake most days (though never in large numbers) the black-capped gull is much in evidence, fighting for scraps or basking on the parapet wall that screens the lake from the road. But now a family of swans is also well established and I expect this gradual spread upwards to continue and some of the medium height lakes to support the growing population of swans on Traeth Mawr. Certainly, they enhance the sylvan beauty of Llyn Mair.

718448 The lake most associated with Blaenau Ffestiniog itself, right in its backyard, so to speak, is Llyn-y-Manod, squeezed in the hollow between Manod Bach and Manod Mawr, the pair of round hills which dominate the eastern side of the town.

705444 The lane to Manod Mawr leads off east at the junction of the Maentwrog and Llan Ffestiniog roads at the south end of Blaenau and soon peters out. Manod Mawr is a great rounded hump, rather like Borrow's Mynydd Mawr standing over Llyn Cwellyn – the path leads north-east from the lane and the route up Manod Mawr actually passes by the side of Llyn-y-Manod.

133

It is a lake without any great character to it, though it is quite a sheet of water, about a quarter-mile long, much beloved by local poachers. The going is pretty wet and the path up Manod Mawr keeps up the flank a bit. But holding more or less to the valley between the two hills, Llyn Du-Bach soon comes into view, overlooking the quarried landscape of east Blaenau. Further on still, round the northern flank of Manod Mawr, two more lakes, Llyn Bowydd and Llyn Newydd, lie on their own plateau.

724468
722470

The sky-line here is superb. To the north is the fine hill of Moel Penamnen, one of the most elegant shapes in Snowdonia. Westward are the Moelwyns and Cnicht, while to the north-west there is a remarkable prospect of the Snowdon Horseshoe which clearly shows the relative heights of the various peaks. A walk round these two lakes can be very wet going. They are in fact reservoirs, captured by fine stone dams. Walking along their northern shore, it is soon apparent that the plateau consists largely of peat.

It is better perhaps to do no more than take in the view, then to complete a circuit round Manod Mawr, taking in Manod slate quarry and its tramway before returning to base by way of Cwm Teigl.

Before leaving the Blaenau Ffestiniog area, there are a few more lakes of great character on its northern side that must not be missed. This involves crossing the Crimea Pass (named not so much after the war as after a public house that once occupied the present car park at the top of the pass – its licence was withdrawn in 1910 after local complaints about the rowdiness of customers and it was demolished in a fit of non-conformist vindictiveness).

695480

As the road ascends to this pass there is a small lake, or rather a reservoir, Llyn Ffridd-y-Bwlch, which must be very familiar to all travellers to and from Blaenau. It has a superb stone-faced dam, since it is yet another quarry reservoir. It is best seen when descending into the town from the east in the evening, and the little lake shimmers like silk against that satanic black quarry face with its attendant waste-tips.

710484

A superb climb on the side opposite Llyn Ffridd-y-Bwlch, straight up the side of the hill, will soon bring Llynnau Barlwyd into view.

702488 Of course, Llynnau Barlwyd can be reached equally well by climbing the hill immediately behind the Crimea car park. From the car park the road descends in the Betws-y-Coed direction in a long dramatic sweep along the flank of the mountain, down into the great bowl of Dolwyddelan – a charming little town, itself a centre for walking and fishing. It has a fine bridge over the Afon Lledr, with lovely water meadows before the river plunges once more down the gorge towards Betws.

In early summer, this vast bowl east of Blaenau Ffestiniog is the haunt of the cuckoo whose monotonous couplet echoes over the rocky humps and marshlands. On occasion, that errant bird can be seen in its straight purposeful flight, attended by the tiny meadow-pipit ('gwas-y-gwcw' in Welsh – cuckoo's servant).

716514 Coming down off the Crimea, there is a steep S-bend and shortly after, a car park on the right. It is also a picnic area by courtesy of the Forestry Commission. Leave the car here (there is a train from Blaenau or Betws for non-drivers) and take the lane opposite
713514 which leads to Roman Bridge station 10 minutes away. The lane has been blasted through solid rock at one stage providing the ideal frame for a view of Siabod's peak. Just after the station the road turns sharply right over the railway and down to a signed bridal path over fields, a beautifully paved path by the way, passing some little boggy patches which are so rich in flora in the Siabod region. The path crosses the road again at a white dormered farmhouse. Follow the path straight up to the left of the farmhouse. Eventually the path becomes a forest trail and carries on over the south-west shoulder of Moel Siabod at about 1,000 feet, with fine views of Eryri over Bwlch Ehediad and even of the Glyders, just peeping over the shoulder between Cribau and Clogwyn Bwlch-y-Maen. The path winds down slowly from the shoulder, debouching on the south-eastern shore of Llyn
685537 Diwaunedd. What a superb lake it is, with the crags of Cribau behind it, and Clogwyn Bwlch-y-Maen to the right. The lake is almost divided into two, not by encroaching deltas but by an intermediate rock barrier, just cut through sufficiently to make one lake. The Ordnance Survey names it Llynnau Diwaunedd. In fine weather it all has that bucolic classical composure that Richard Wilson sought so studiously at Llyn Cau on Cader Idris. In winter, this area can be locked in the grip of ice and snow and the Crimea has days when it is impassable. Diwaunedd is then austere and lonely.

The Forestry Commission has been discreet about planting, taking their rows to the foot of the lake only, and leaving the rest of the shoreline clear. I hope they have no plans to change this state of affairs, because Llyn Diwaunedd is a fine lake which could suffer by planting all round.

Diwaunedd may be deceiving in terms of distance and time, and what looks like little more than two miles on the map can take over two hours going up. The terrain is far from level, a rest at the lake is necessary, so altogether the excursion is a long afternoon's walk, especially if things like the spotted orchid are to be enjoyed on the way. The Forestry road from the lake leads back to Roman Bridge, by the way, but is not half as attractive as the bridle path.

Lastly, in this highly interesting Dolwyddelan area, there is Llyn y Foel to be visited before the road carries on to Betws.

Shortly after leaving Dolwyddelan, the main road bears left and very soon there is a public footpath signed to the left. This path almost at once debouches on to a wide forest trail, climbs across an old quarry face in a loop, then plunges into the forest. Unlike the Betws-y-Coed area, this trail is not guided by signs, so the walker can be dazed by a multiplicity of choices of direction. The aim is to get to the north-west corner of the forest, and in general, the sharp and rather tempting off-shoots left should be avoided, while guarding against going too far right. The straightforward route crosses the stream twice, and about a hundred yards after the second crossing the road left gradually swings round and uphill to that north-west corner, where, surprisingly after the previous dearth of signs, the Forestry Commission has obligingly placed a pointer and sign saying 'Courtesy path to Moel Siabod'.

Leaving the forest by the usual ladder–stile, the path now leads directly upstream towards the cascading outflow of Llyn y Foel, high above under the folds and crags of Moel Siabod. Once again, this is a classic corrie, with the lip to be climbed, among boulders and debris, until the top is reached, and there, across some forty yards of lip, is Llyn y Foel.

715548

Once the entire corrie comes into view this lake reveals itself as one of the finest. First, the synclinal rock barrier at its foot is beautifully delineated, as though the slabs and layers had cooled and crystallized only recently. Then the ridge behind the lake, superb granite slabs ascending to the summit, is surely one of the most conspicuous in the area. Once again, it is the lake in its context that impresses. Two rocky islets enhance the lake. A small dam (now ruined) at the rock barrier once raised the height of the lake, but now the lake is all very much as nature made it.

The long walk through the forest and the climb up to the lip of the corrie make the lake sufficient destination, but the more athletic will feel challenged by the ridge leading up to the summit. Moel Siabod, at 2,850 feet above sea level, is one of the best viewpoints in Snowdonia. Walking from the summit along the broad ridge of grass and boulders brings the Glyders, Tryfan, the Carneddau and Cwm Llugwy into view. Lakes abound, with Llynnau Mymbyr directly below, and to the east, several of the many sheets of water round Betws-y-Coed, notably Llyn Elsi in the forest over the town.

Descending the east shoulder of Siabod is not easy, and a return to the summit and a descent down the ridge to the lake is the simplest way back. But a full circuit is possible, down to a quarry pool in a very interesting worked-out area of pale grey slates and shales, taking in two isolated lakes on the grassy plateau that feed Afon Llugwy, and then skirting round over rather difficult heather and bog back to Llyn y Foel.

In all, this circuit constitutes one of the more strenuous and exciting walks, so it is important to confine it to good weather and to take all day over it.

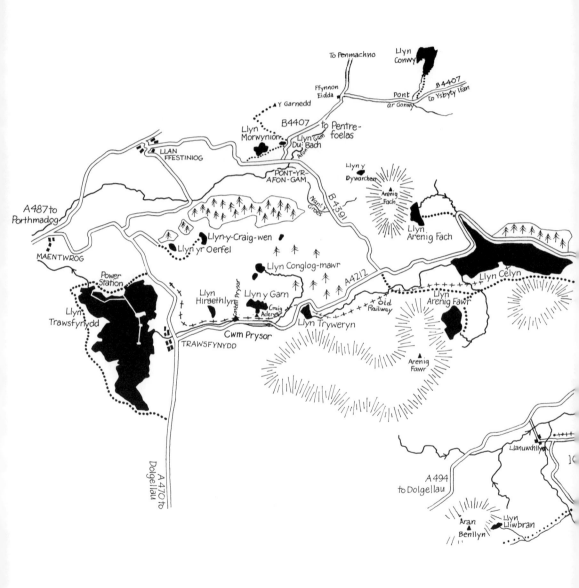

Ten Llan Ffestiniog to Bala

705420   East of Llan Ffestiniog (I note the 'Llan' is omitted on the latest O.S. maps, but locally the 'Llan' and the 'Blaenau' are very much in use to distinguish the two Ffestiniogs, and if in a street conversation in Porthmadog the word 'Ffestiniog' cropped up, Blaenau would be inferred, though Llan is the older) there is a wide expanse with more lakes on the way to Bala. The road (B4391) out of Llan used to be the main route across this country, but since the building of the atomic power station at Traws-fynydd, a new road (A4212), built mainly over an old drover's road, has superseded it as the main road from Porthmadog to

710355
950390   Bala. So there are three points to the triangle that fairly covers this territory and its lakes; Llan Ffestiniog and Trawsfynydd to the west and Bala to the east.

735417   Taking the old route out of Llan Ffestiniog towards Bala, there is first a deep ravine to the right of the road, with the Cynfal Falls cascading over a precipice, before the land rolls out into a moorland of bog and heather.

745419   The highest filling station in Wales, Pont-yr-Afon-Gam, 'Bridge of the Crooked River', at over 1,200 feet marks an interesting diversion for lake-walkers. For here, a road departs left at right-angles for Penmachno and Ysbyty Ifan. True to the stream's name, the road twists about uphill and not far on to the

745425   left is a small lake, Llyn Du-Bach – oval shaped and almost featureless except as the foreground to a view of the Moelwyns. A favourite stopping place for motorists, it is a prelude to a larger lake of some consequence in Welsh legend. For the rough road that climbs up beside Llyn Du-Bach offers a view higher up of

737424   Llyn Morwynion to the south-west, otherwise hidden from the

main road. Llyn Morwynion, 'Lake of the Maidens', probably .
denotes the place where Blodeuedd and her Maidens of Ardudwy
drowned while fleeing from Gwydion and the men of Gwynedd.

> Gwydion travelled in the forefront and made for Mur Castell.
> Blodeuedd heard that they were coming, took her maidens
> with her and made for the mountains, and over Cynfal river
> they made for a court that was on the mountain. But through
> fear they could not proceed save with their faces looking
> backwards. And then, never a thing knew they before they fell
> into the lake, and were all drowned save she alone. And then
> Gwydion overtook her too, and he said to her: 'I will not slay
> thee, I will do thee that which is worse; That is,' he said, 'I will
> let thee go in the form of a bird' . . .

And so Blodeuedd became Blodeuwedd (Flower-Face), which is
a name given, appropriately enough, to the owl.

But Pennant tells another version, of the Men of Ardudwy
raiding Clwyd and carrying off wives for themselves. The Men of
Clwyd followed and slew the raiders at Beddau Gwyr Ardudwy,
'Graves of the Men of Ardudwy'. The women had already
established themselves so well in the affections of their new
companions that they flung themselves in despair into the waters
of Llyn Morwynion. So the legend goes, but I should have
thought the motive was more fear of facing their own men from
Clwyd after such a quick change of affection!

That view of Llyn Morwynion from above is probably the best,
though it is some distance from the lake itself. But it surveys that
entire terrain of Blodeuedd's flight. The lake lies in its green
hollow amid the upland above Cynfal, and across the way,
looking south-west, Llyn Trawsfynydd and the heights of
Ardudwy. The road leads on to old quarry workings near a
magnificent dome of rock called Y Garnedd. Depending on the
day, this can be one of the greatest prospects of Wales. Further on
there used to be two more lakes called Llynnau Gamallt, still
shown on some maps, but nothing except swampland now. They
do not appear on the first Ordnance Survey.

Back on the Pont-yr-Afon-Gam road, opposite Llyn Du-Bach, lies the spoil heap of another old quarry. How those nineteenth-century fellows speculated – and often lost! The heap actually straddles the stream of Afon-Gam and below it there is a sight worth seeking out. The stream leaps over a 20 foot overhang into a deep green pool. Hidden from the road, it is a jewel of uncelebrated glory.

From Llyn Du-Bach, the road climbs and twists and then levels out and straightens on the rolling moorland. Nearly two miles out from Pont-yr-Afon-Gam, an old cattle drovers' well called Ffynnon Eidda and a signpost mark the bifurcation to Penmachno and Ysbyty Ifan respectively. Three miles along the Ysbyty Ifan road there is a dip over a bridge, Pont-ar-Gonwy, which is near the source of the River Conwy. The river falls to the right under the bridge and after a series of cascades continues to Ysbyty Ifan, Betws-y-Coed and ultimately the sea at Conwy.

762437

778447

For the lake-walker who drives to his base, there is a convenient car park in an old roadside quarry on the left shortly after the bridge and just before a lonely house, rarely occupied. A rough track (fortunately debarred to motor traffic) leads northwards out of the quarry through a gate. There is no hint of a lake, only gently rising moorland, peat, heather, sphagnum (which here flourishes a brilliant green in striking contrast to the deep browns all round). It is wild, sportsman's country. The half-bark, half-growl of a rising grouse can be disconcerting to the merely aesthetic. Less than a mile from the quarry the track debouches quite unexpectedly on an open stretch of water, Llyn Conwy.

780460

Here is an example of water catchment on a high plateau. All round the leets and rivulets gather the rainfall and fill this gentle dip in the land nearly 1,500 feet above sea level. There are no trees, only heather and bog as far as the eye can see, with a fine view of Moel Siabod away to the north. Llyn Conwy is an angler's lake and there is a hut for that single-minded fraternity's private use. A small parapet, hardly a dam, controls the outflow. The level has not changed since the early nineteenth century Ordnance Survey. A little off-shore, a small, weather-bleached islet of rock provides a foothold for immaculately white sea-birds, and it is quite likely that walkers will find a dunlin or two not far from their feet. Possibly they are used to scraps from the anglers.

This diversion from Pont-yr-Afon-Gam is well worth the trouble for those who do not feel desolate on a high open moorland. It is very like the Wicklow Hills in Ireland; when I walk there, I half expect to stumble over 'turf' (the Irish never call it peat). Borrow records that he saw peat stacks here, but there are no diggings now. Either the peat is not the right kind for fuel, or the Welsh are either unaware of the virtues of this inestimable material or too well endowed by Welsh coal to bother. Even the eerie signpost at Ffynnon Eidda has the air of the 'Troubles'. I remember painting a water-colour there when the signpost, set against a storm cloud, might have been a gibbet. The whole area is so different from the vernal richness of Nant Gwynant that it gives further indication of the extent of the contrast between individual lakes in North Wales.

759410
762420
A mile from Pont-yr-Afon-Gam in the Bala direction, the road crosses a stream at Nant-y-Groes. Nearly a mile upstream into the moors lies Llyn-y-Dywarchen, source of the Afon Cynfal, not to be confused with its namesake of the 'floating island' near Rhyd-Ddu.

Footbridge: Llyn Trawsfynydd

But to continue along the road to Bala, no lakes occur as far as
818395   Arenig. Here the road joins the new Trawsfynydd road (A4212),
so it is a junction that can be reached by either the old B4391 from
Llan Ffestiniog or an eight-mile walk from Trawsfynydd, either
by the new road or along the old railway.

710355   The old Welsh village of Trawsfynydd means different things to
different people. Basically it is just a roadside village on the main
route northwards from Dolgellau to Ffestiniog, and a new
by-pass now leaves it behind somewhat. But the Romans must
706387   have known the area, for their station at Tomen-y-Mur is just
over a field or two. Rising from the coastal area below
Maentwrog, Trawsfynydd was the first settlement on the way
south. And travelling from England via Bala, it was the first
settlement beyond the mountains (hence its name – 'Over the
Mountain'). The drovers would know it well after the long climb
up from the coast and from the Vale of Maentwrog. Any Welsh
man or woman worth their salt knows that it was the home of the
shepherd poet Hedd Wyn, who won the National Eisteddfod
Chair in 1916 but did not survive the holocaust of the Western
Front to receive it. Outside the chapel in the middle of the village
his statue stands in proud memory of this man of peace who died
at war. Roman Catholics revere the area as the birthplace of St
John Roberts who died for his faith during Elizabeth's reign. For
railway enthusiasts, Trawsfynydd was a station on the old line
that left Ruabon on the London line and traversed the mountains
via Bala and Arenig, and was drowned in the making of Llyn
Celyn (about which more follows).

In 1838 when the first Ordnance Survey of the area was published
there was no lake at Trawsfynydd. There was only an extensive
bog known as Cors Goch (Red Bog) held back by Craig Gyfynys
which hangs over Maentwrog, and drained by Afon Llenyrch.

The lake first came into existence as recently as 1926, as a reservoir
after the dam was built over the outflow of Afon Llenyrch. Before
that Cors Goch drained off down a deep gorge, over rock
platforms and enormous boulders, and must have been a dramatic
water-course in its time, especially during a spate. Now it is only
a trickle. The water was piped down from the dam to the
Maentwrog Power Station on the floor of the valley below. The
walk from the new Atomic Power Station public car park to the

dam is about 1½ miles and is a bracing hour there and back across a good stretch of country at nearly 600 feet above sea level.

The building of the atomic power station made little difference to the lake, except to raise its temperature and to introduce a circular flow round its perimeter by baffle walls connecting the islands, to direct the warmed water from the station after its use as a coolant. Mr White, the Station Manager, told me that they reckoned it took eight days for this induced current to complete the circuit round the lake, which gives some measure of its extent. It is nearly 3 miles long and 1½ miles at its widest. The raised temperature has its uses. At the fish farm – a fascinating sight itself – lovely fat Rainbow trout feeding in their thousands in circular tanks are brought to maturity earlier than usual by the extra degree or two. This fish farm is just along the first barrier wall to the left of the public car park and is on the public footpath to the old dam.

Llyn Trawsfynydd is a very public lake. Not only does it provide the coolant for the power station but it is one of the most popular fishing locations for the angling community. The Central Electricity Board fosters this carefully. Its fish farm stocks not only Llyn Trawsfynydd, but other reservoirs like Llyn-y-Stradau and Llyn Rheidol. In addition, a nature trail has been laid and parties are also shown round the station and its environment by appointment. Care was taken with the planting when the station was built, Miss Sylvia Crowe, the landscape artist, acting as consultant. Access to the lake is easy (the station itself is another matter, of course). Walks all round the lake are well worth while, especially for the views; to the south the great spine of Ardudwy careening away, with a distant backdrop of Cader Idris; westwards the pyramid of Arenig Fawr, most impressive in winter when it is almost always capped by an unbroken cover of snow; northwards the Moelwyns on the far side of the Vale of Ffestiniog.

The best start to an excursion round the lake begins in the village, at an access road on the way south down the main street from Hedd Wyn's monument. It winds over to the lake and to a quarter-mile-long footbridge which crosses the head of the lake.

Trawsfynydd also provides a quite separate springboard for the route to Bala with a grand excursion up the old railway, winding all the way up Cwm Prysor, clinging to the slopes, crossing deep stream-beds by marvellous stone bridges of consummate skill in masonry (the granite came either from Arenig or from a small isolated quarry on the side of Llyn Conglog-mawr) or being crossed by others to connect farm land, and finally, quite near the watershed at Tryweryn, negotiating the deep cutting of Afon Prysor by a superb viaduct. Some of the best walking in North Wales lies along abandoned railway lines. Those old 'navigators' had a genius for landscape and this abandoned Ffestiniog–Bala line is superb. In fact it went further, of course, to link up with the main line at Ruabon, but these are sore memories and best left aside while we enjoy excursions along the ballast and turf of their surfaces.

743370   Between Trawsfynydd and Tryweryn, the meres of Llyn
760377   Hiraethlyn and Llyn y Garn lie just off the railway line on its
            northern flank, while a little further north over the moors Llyn
760388   Conglog-mawr provides the source of Afon Prysor.

The first, Llyn Hiraethlyn, was described by Humphrey Llwyd in 1584 as 'Llyn y Ithlyn which abounds with a very peculiar perch which hath a twist in ye tale and choice trouts'. The perch are still there, I understand, but by now are disgustingly normal. Remembering all the tales of one-eyed fish and others with monstrous heads and so on in so many Welsh lakes, one day an angler is going to bring out the oddest monster of all, and being an angler, nobody is going to believe him.

Llyn Hiraethlyn lies in a quiet hollow, about two miles up Cwm Prysor and not more than a hundred yards from the railway line on the left.

Llynnau y Garn and Conglog-mawr are not so easy, but well worth a day's hard trek. Half-way up Cwm Prysor the railway skirts round the bastion of Craig Aderyn, high above the road in a way that railway engineers seem always to have enjoyed, rather as they circumnavigated the cliffs of the Rockies or the foothills of the Himalayas. It is still obvious why Craig Aderyn earned its name, for as soon as you start to scale its side, a kestrel will start screaming at you and will not stop until you have left his eyrie. But Craig Aderyn must be scaled somehow and it is rough heather and scree on a very steep gradient all the way up. Down below, rising from the valley floor, the isolated tump of Castell Prysor is clearly defined, like a hill fortress guarding the pass. Its history, if any, is obscure.

There is a little cairn atop Craig Aderyn and the view all round is spectacular: to the south, Cader Idris blue on the skyline; then Y Llethr and the Rhinogs, followed by Llyn Trawsfynydd and Llyn Hiraethlyn due west below; the Lleyn Peninsula stretching away into gold and silver behind them, and round to the heights of Snowdon; then right over the moors to the north and finally the broken ridge of the Arenigs to the east, with Llyn y Garn for a splendid foreground.

Llyn y Garn is complex in shape, scooped out of the hard rock. Thick, tangled heather covers the rock down to the shore. The waters are practically bare of vegetation.

Old Ffestiniog–Bala railway line

Arenig Fawr from Llyn
Tryweryn

The best route to Llyn Conglog-mawr is to head for the
power-lines that cross the moors here. It is still rough humpy
country, rather like walking over a feather mattress at times, the
heather is so impenetrable. A few brace of grouse will still rise, a
memory of days when this whole territory was regarded as good
rough shooting. But Llyn Conglog-mawr is really worthwhile,
since it contrasts so strongly with its neighbour. It is really two
lakes, the smaller coming into view first, separated from the
larger one by a heather-covered hump. Both lakes are silting up
and though this renders the smaller one of little interest, the larger
one, being only half-covered, is rather beautiful. The reeds and
grasses ripple in the wind, and in high summer the white
water-lily blooms at the edge near the outflow. But that is not all.
The outflow itself passes through a charming shallow pool before
descending in its long curve round to Cwm Prysor. This pool is
graced by the yellow water-lily, the 'Brandy-bottle'. Now in
many lakes, like Llyn Mwyngil and Tecwyn Isaf, the white and
the yellow flourish together. But there is no doubt about it: at
Llyn Conglog-mawr the white flourishes only in the lake, and the

yellow only in the outflow pool. And nowhere, I think, have I seen such pure gold against such pellucid black. For this sight, it is worth planning the excursion in July or August.

The return to the railway line is as rough as ever, but the rest of the walk along the line, crossing the spectacular viaduct over Afon 789386 Prysor, is simple as far as Llyn Tryweryn at the watershed.

Travellers from Trawsfynydd, when they reach the watershed (just where the railway line crosses the new road) will find Tryweryn with ease, for it occupies the level top of the pass. Just round it, the new road actually takes the course of the old railway.

These watershed lakes are quite common in Wales. After a steep climb to a pass there is often a flat tableland pitted either with small pools or with a single tarn of some character. Tryweryn is typical.

In winter the road is often impassable, and in 1978–9 the lake was frozen over for quite a long spell. Augustus John and J. D. Innes travelled this way in their North Wales safari. Innes, already suffering from pulmonary tuberculosis, can't have found the going very comfortable. He certainly paused at Llyn Tryweryn to paint the superb little canvas now in the National Museum of Wales. Borrow passed nearby on the Ffestiniog–Bala road, stopping at Tai-Hirion on the way for a drink of water, and the lady of the house probably told Borrow a whopper about Llyn Tryweryn. When Borrow asked her about the lake over the way and, as usual, about the fish in it, she answered: 'Digon, Sir, digon iawn, and some very large. I once saw a Pen-hwyad from that lake which weighed fifty-pounds.' But it is just possible that she was right, for a pen-hwyad (literally 'duck-head') is a pike.

From Llyn Tryweryn the road winds down (or better still, of course, continues along the old railway line, which curves down and finally debouches into the new Llyn Celyn) to the flat bogland near the Ffestiniog–Bala road junction. This flatland under the shadow of Arenig Fawr and its granite roadstone quarry must once have been a lake. Typical factors in its disappearance are all too evident: first the silting up with debris and alluvial drift from the slopes all round, and secondly the outflowing river cutting a channel through the rock barrier at its foot, thus draining it.

The two Arenigs, Fawr and Fach, stand either side of the valley, each with a forbidding corrie on the east side, holding a lake. The pyramidal western slopes of Arenig Fawr to the right of the road tend to hold the snow in winter and glisten on a January afternoon when viewed from the far west. Arenig Fach on the north side is more a hog-back ridge.

817395 At the junction of the Ffestiniog road with the Trawsfynydd one, there is a metalled lane opposite leading to the granite roadstone quarries, and after about one and a half miles, just above the head of Llyn Celyn, a path leads right steeply up the slopes towards the corrie under Arenig Fawr's east face. It is in fact an old quarry road, now disused and covered with springy green turf, and 850380 provides an easy route direct to Llyn Arenig Fawr. All round, heather or rushes discourage wandering, and small spoil heaps, now mostly overgrown, indicate the reason for the road in the past.

The climb is a fair gradient at first, with fine views backwards over the head of Llyn Celyn, then levels out as the corrie comes into view over the shoulder. The full round lake is reached in about twenty minutes all told, so cannot be counted as one of the more strenuous excursions.

The green 'road' ends at the head of Llyn Arenig Fawr, but the sheep, or a succession of walkers (for it is a popular excursion for walkers from Bala, ever a happy hunting ground for travellers like Borrow) have trodden a clear path on the left of the lake, through the tangled heather. From this path the lake in sunshine can take on a peacock blue hue, contrasting with the wide broken corrie beyond, and the two huge *roches moutonnées* that must once have arrested and divided the glacier tearing at the steep slopes.

Llyn Arenig Fawr is a reservoir, with a fine stone-faced dam at its foot. Now that Llyn Celyn efficiently controls the waters in this area the sluice is out of commission and its steel housing has been flung unceremoniously on the grass below. A walk over the dam leads by a fairly easy shoulder up to the summit of Arenig Fawr, a mountain I have always felt is tinged with sadness, for near the top stands a monument to the crew of an American Fortress Bomber which crashed here after completing a mission during the war. Molten metal and scrap still litter the bare inhospitable terrain.

Llyn Celyn

845419

830415

From the dam southwards the moors stretch away to a distant view of Aran Fawddwy. Unless a long traverse is contemplated over the moors south-east towards Bala, it is best to return from Llyn Arenig Fawr by the same path to the Ffestiniog-Trawsfynydd junction, where the Bala road proceeds to Llyn Celyn and bears left across the head of the lake to a sharp turn over a bridge. This bridge marks the departure point for Llyn Arenig Fach. A gated path to the left rises towards the shoulder under the hog-back of Arenig Fach. Although there is no marked path the corrie ahead is all too apparent and once the brow is reached, there it is, a matter of half-an-hour from the main road, a long oval lake lying across the corrie with its outflow to the north. It is a depleted lake, with once submerged boulders now bleaching in the weather. These boulders are of a strange complexity, with colours ranging from warm pinks and blue-greys to the pure white of quartz. For some reason, I find Llyn Arenig Fach the more interesting of the two Arenigs, perhaps because it seems more remote and wild, though it is no further from the road. Like its partner over the valley it too was once a reservoir with a similar stone-faced dam and sluice, the abandoned steel housing of which now careens at an acute angle to its cylindrical plinth, looking from a distance like some strange space instrument polarized on the North Star. Most of all, however, Llyn Arenig Fach is a fine place for wheatears, beautiful little upland birds which dart from boulder to boulder, chattering as they go and seeming to take pleasure in darting on their delicate pins out of sight behind the boulders and then, as you think you have lost them, flitting out again to the next perch.

The outflow from the dam (it seems to seep under the now broken stonework) appears to present an inviting way back to the bridge, but lower down this route is very marshy indeed so it is advisable to return more or less the same way. Well-shod ornithologists who do keep to the stream will find much to interest them, not least the dipper darting blackly over the surface of the water.

Llyn Arenig Fach

Dam: Llyn Celyn

So, back to Llyn Celyn, which not so many years ago was a marshy valley.

I remember the steam train that traversed this old land, till twenty years ago, from Blaenau Ffestiniog up through Cwm Prysor, over Tryweryn and by the side of the bogland under Arenig and on to Bala.

That was a period when important environmental decisions were being made and implemented – the atomic power station at Trawsfynydd and a reservoir at Capel Celyn to control the flow of the River Dee for Liverpool and Deeside. This flat bogland figured in the deliberations, I am sure, and certainly a dam over the original rock barrier would have restored the lake which I presume once existed after the Ice Age. It would not have necessitated the drowning of a village which is a basic Welsh trauma. At any rate, the next step down to this valley, across another boggy area (as it was then), provided the water engineers with a better solution.

850405   It meant drowning Capel Celyn. As with many of these boggy areas in a valley, it can be assumed that after the melting of the glaciers, Celyn held a lake until its overflow cut through the rock barrier at its foot. A grass dam over this rock barrier was the solution, and under some protest – *Cofiwch Tryweryn* ('Remember Tryweryn') after the river that flowed through the valley – up went the dam and away for ever went the village and the railway. Llyn Celyn once again existed.

Nobody will count the cost now. It may be forgiven, but it will never be forgotten. There *was* a cost. Capel Celyn was never much of a village to look at, but it was an old community, not easily dismissed in the annals of Welsh Nonconformity and its tradition.

The area had a habit of breeding characters, like Bob Tai'r Felin the folk-singer who died not twenty years ago. The former community and the dead in its drowned graveyard are now remembered in R. L. Gapper's worthy lakeside chapel, an austere monument built of glacial boulders and slate. Another drowned memory is the former presence of Quakers in this valley. They too are commemorated in a fine bronze plaque, also by Gapper, set into an enormous boulder at the lay-by near the dam.

Now that the trees are beginning to flourish along the north shore, Llyn Celyn at over two miles long is becoming a fine lake, except in droughty seasons like 1976, when its level gets so low it leaves an unsightly shore-line of silt. It is a motorist's lake with ample lay-bys. And, of course, our old friends the anglers love it too. Long may they flourish – they may be cagey about walkers and they are all too ready to fence off lakes with barbed wire, but as long as their sportsman's privilege and privacy are paramount, so long will the dreadful power-boats and water-skiers be held back, and the pristine nature of the lakes maintained.

But even as I write, there is a threat that the power-boats and the skiers will be permitted at Llyn Celyn. Long may it be resisted!

Opposite Rhaeadr Cynfal

Continuing along the road to Bala, the problem is all too evident at Wales's largest lake, Llyn Tegid, nearly four miles long and very tempting to some of the noisier lake-users. Fortunately, the local authorities have so far forbidden the launching of power-boats on the lake and, if anything, the sailing dinghies that scud across its surface enhance its beauty in summertime. So the problem of Windermere and its water-skiers has been avoided sensibly so far.

Llyn Tegid is a fine lake, especially viewed from its foot with the ridge of Aran, nearly 3,000 feet high, beyond and further still the tops of Cader Idris. Tegid lies in the rift valley that extends from north-east to south-west in this area, down ultimately to Tal-y-Llyn and the sea at Tywyn.

Llyn Tegid (or Llyn-y-Bala, as it is sometimes called after the town at its foot) lies at 529 feet above sea level and has a maximum depth of 136 feet. The depth has been slightly lowered with the Dee water storage scheme, but beyond the loss to botanists of the sedge that used to grow in some of its inlets, it has not substantially changed the lake in its appearance or its ecology. There are extensive areas of alluvial drift at either end, helping to hold the lake in this great rift valley. The Romans extended their Welsh connection along this rift, not merely to enjoy lake walking by Llyn Tegid and Tal-y-Llyn, but to exploit the minerals in the surrounding hills, even gold near the head of the lake at Llanuwchllyn. This through route from the Vale of Cheshire to the heartland of Wales has enabled travellers through the ages to see more of Llyn Tegid than of any other Welsh lake and to record their observations.

Humphrey Llwyd in his *History of Cambria* (1584) notes that there was 'a kind of fish called *gwyniad* which are like the whitings'. This fact seems to have impressed subsequent travellers who, I would guess, never saw a *gwyniad*.

However, in 1756, Lord George Lyttleton of Hagley in Worcestershire noted more than the *gwyniad*: 'What Bala is most famous for is the beauty of its women, and indeed I saw there some of the prettiest girls I ever beheld.' Even so, he preferred the flavour of the *gwyniad* 'to the lips of the fair maids of Bala'.

Another fish unique in this area to Llyn Tegid is the grayling, introduced some time since 1770, though apparently many other species absent from most North Wales lakes survive in Tegid – like roach, rudd, chub, pike, loach, etc.

Pennant regarded Tegid as:

> a fine expanse of water nearly four miles long and twelve hundred yards broad at the widest part; the deepest part is opposite Bryn Goleu where it is 46 yards deep, with three yards of mud; the shores gravelly; the boundaries are easy slopes, well cultivated and varied with woods. In stormy weather its billows are run very high . . .

> . . . It rises sometimes nine feet and rain and winds jointly contribute to make it overflow the fair vale of Edeirnion.

> . . . Its fish are pike, perch, trout, a few roach, and abundance of eels; and shoals of that Alpine fish, the Gwyniad, which spawn in December and are taken in great numbers in spring or summer. Pike have been caught here of twenty-five pounds weight, a trout of twenty-two, a perch of ten and a gwyniad of five.

This latter being of course yet more anglers' tales, Sir Herbert Maxwell in 1904 was sceptical: 'Pennant was a good naturalist, no doubt; but he was even more renowned as a traveller, whose business it was to make his tales readable. He may have refrained, therefore, from making due allowance for that remarkable property in sporting fish which causes them to increase continuously in weight after death.'

As for the fluctuation in the lake's level of nine feet and the billows running high: this latter fact is well known to present-day yachtsmen on the lake, where capsizing is apparently part of the fun. The Dee scheme has domesticated the level to a boring consistency.

The effect of all this human activity on wild-life is difficult to assess. Llyn Tegid was never a favourite haunt of ornithologists, according to Condry, since its vegetation is mostly inadequate to support surface-feeding duck. Mallard, pochard, tufted duck and golden-eye are just about the sum of them, he says. 'Whooper swans irregularly, usually in hard weather; cormorants regularly, especially immatures; and of course herons' complete his list of lake birds.

Llyn Tegid is associated with the old Welsh patriarch, Llewarch Hen. This was meat and drink to the indefatigable Borrow who might be best left to tell the story in his own way:

> Llewarch Hen, or Llewarch the Aged, was born about the commencement of the sixth and died about the middle of the seventh century, having attained to the prodigious age of one hundred and forty or fifty years, which is perhaps the lot of about forty individuals in the course of a millennium. If he was remarkable for the number of his years he was no less remarkable for the number of his misfortunes. He was one of the princes of the Cumbrian Britons; but Cumbria was invaded by the Saxons, and a scene of horrid war ensued. Llewarch and his sons, of whom he had twenty-four, put themselves at the head of their forces, and in conjunction with the other Cumbrian princes made a brave but fruitless opposition to the invaders. Most of his sons were slain, and he himself with the remainder sought shelter in Powys in the hall of Cynddylan its prince. But the Saxon bills and bows found their way to Powys too. Cynddylan was slain, and with him the last of the sons of Llewarch, who, reft of his protector, retired to a hut by the side of the lake of Bala, where he lived the life of a recluse and composed elegies on his sons and slaughtered friends, and on his old age, all of which abound with so much simplicity and pathos that the heart of him must be hard indeed who can read them unmoved. Whilst a prince he was revered for his wisdom and equity, and he is said in one of the historical triads to have been one of the consulting warriors of Arthur.

Another traveller, A. G. Bradley, seemed impressed more by the tradition for 'Grouse, theology and cwrw-dda' (good ale), but he does have time to mention the lake: 'There is sailing and boating in plenty on the lake, though no steamers or steam-launches are haply permitted to ply upon it.' And as usual, he goes on to talk about the fish, and the sad tale of the *gwyniad*, which, 'when hunted by the fierce pike, fling themselves in their panic on to the gravelly strand and die there, unable to get back'. Interestingly enough, Bradley was stepping into the current controversy, for if it is not 'steam-launches', it is now power-boats.

Higher up the lake at Glanllyn, Urdd Gobaith Cymru (The Welsh League of Youth) has an estate for outdoor pursuits, and is one of the mainsprings of the Welsh way of life. Indeed this whole area, despite the dominance of tourist traffic from the last century onwards, remains among the most Welsh areas of Wales. Just above the head of the lake on the Dolgellau road, the village of Llanuwchllyn has become a sort of preserve of Welshness. Here, at the entrance to the village, stands the monument to two of its most illustrious sons. Sir Owen Morgan Edwards, an Oxford don who at the beginning of the century relinquished that most rewarding of stations to become a School Inspector in Wales, in order to assist at the revival of the Welsh language after many years of repression of the tongue; and his son, Sir Ifan ap Owen Edwards, who founded Urdd Gobaith Cymru. The monument is built of Arenig granite and the figures, in bronze, were by the present writer.

873303

Ffynnon Eidda

Llanuwchllyn is also the starting-point for an interesting way of viewing the lake in the summer season, for here yet another of Wales's little railways begins, Rheilffordd Llyn Tegid (Bala Lake Narrow Gauge Railway). The line hugs the south-east shore of the lake as far as Bala.

Llyn Tegid, perhaps because of its extent, is connected with one of those inborn legends in Welsh tradition, of the drowned city. In 1860 Hugh Humphrey published it in this form:

> Tradition relates that Bala Lake is but the watery tomb of the palaces of iniquity, and that some boatmen . . . can hear at times a feeble voice saying 'Vengeance will come, Vengeance will come', and another voice enquiring 'When will it come?' The first voice answers, 'In the third generation.' Those voices were a recollection over oblivion of an oppressive and cruel prince who used frequently to hear a voice saying 'Vengeance will come', but he always laughed the threat away with reckless contempt. One night a poor harper . . . was ordered to come to the prince's palace. About midnight, when there was an interval in the dancing and the old harper had been left alone in a corner, he suddenly heard a voice saying in a sort of whisper in his ear, 'Vengeance, Vengeance'. He turned at once and saw a little bird hovering above him, beckoning him, as it were, to follow.

F. J. North develops this theme at length in his book *Sunken Cities* published by the University of Wales Press in 1957. North goes on to recount how the bird enticed the old harper up to the top of a hill. When he decided it was time to return to the palace, he looked and found no trace of it; it was all now a lake, 'and his harp was floating on the calm surface of the water'.

This Welsh version of Sodom and Gomorrah is basic to Welsh feeling. The drowned city keeps recurring, even as late as the age of film-making, with Emlyn Williams keening over the 'Last Days of Dolwen'. Yet it is, as we have seen, also a reality, for the loss of Capel Celyn represented a wound that cannot be understood on the other side of Offa's Dyke.

Old Borrow, ever the keen Cymrophile, tried his best and in *Wild Wales* he records a dialogue he has with a local lad:

> *Myself* – Bala is a nice place.
> *Lad* – It is, Sir; but not so fine as old Bala.
> *Myself* – I never heard of such a place. Where is it?
> *Lad* – Under the lake, Sir.
> *Myself* – What do you mean?
> *Lad* – It stood in the old time where the lake now is, and a fine city it was, full of fine houses, towers and castles, but with neither church nor chapel, for the people neither knew God nor cared for Him, and thought of nothing but singing and dancing and other wicked things. So God was angry, and one night when they were all busy at singing and dancing and the like, God gave the word and the city sank down into the Unknown, and the lake boiled up where it once stood.

North is a little less credulous than Borrow, or do I underestimate Borrow, who does not often append his reactions to these tales, but merely records them and leaves us to draw our own conclusions? North on this particular tale quotes W. Bingley's *Tour of North Wales, performed during the Summer of 1798.*

> The overflowings of this pool [Llyn Tegid] are at times very dreadful; but this seldom happens, except when the winds rush from the mountains, when they drive the waters before them, even over the great part of the Vale of Edeirnion, rising in stormy weather very suddenly from the joint force of the winds and mountain torrents, sometimes eight or nine feet in perpendicular height and almost threatening the town with destruction.

North points out that, as the map shows, Bala lies at the end of a lake well situated to be affected by south-westerly gales. The present control of the height of the lake has dealt with this danger and the town of Bala is now no longer inundated by storm water. But one can imagine that hellfire sermons of the early part of last century would do much to perpetuate a Sodom and Gomorrah legend in the locality. Even today Bala is still a strong evangelical centre, but its college for the training of ministers is closed and the innocuous antics of the sailing dinghies are all that can be seen on the lake and 'Vengeance, Vengeance,' seems far away.

At the head of Llyn Tegid the ridge of Aran Benllyn and Aran Fawddwy dominates the skyline. Oddly enough, while many people think Cader Idris is second only to Yr Wyddfa in height and drama, Aran Fawddwy at 2,974 feet is 50 feet higher than Cader.

However, these actual heights are of no direct concern to lake-walkers, except that heights usually mean mass, and mass as often as not means a stretch of water of some kind in an associated valley or hollow. Aran Benllyn is worth a great deal of trouble, for a corrie lake, Llyn Lliwbran, lies under the east face of its ridge. It is the only lake we shall consider that is south of the Bala-Talyllyn Fault, but since it flows into Llyn Tegid, it seems right and proper to consider it as part of our territory.

895270

The eastern flank of Aran Benllyn is reached by taking the road out of Llanuwchllyn (about 1½ miles above the head of Llyn Tegid) up the valley of Cwm Cynllwyd as far as Talardd (about 2 miles up the cwm). A lane on the right at Talardd leads up a tributary valley, Cwm Croes, and after somewhat more than a mile once more to the right, the flank of Aran Benllyn rises quite steeply. It is a case of following the stream up to the corrie.

One of the first concerns of this area is its botany, if we are to take note of that earliest of enthusiasts, Edward Lluyd, who wrote to his cousin, David Lloyd, thus in 1686: 'Aran Benllyn is I hear too far from you, else I am sure you might find there twice as many plants as on [the Berwyn]. Divers gentlemen have gone from London, Oxford and Cambridge to Snowdon, Cader Idris and Flinlimmon in search of plants; but I find there were never many at Aran Benllyn: the reason I suppose may be because it is not so famous for height as the aforementioned hills, but to my knowledge it produces as many rarities as Cader Idris.' In particular, Lluyd was referring to 'ye rivulets that run through ye rocks above Llyn Llymbran'.

875254

Although the name given to the lake is that still often used by locals, the Ordnance Survey today refers to it as Llyn Lliwbran, which Condry suggests could be incorrect, and I would agree with him. For on these matters I would always trust a local before I trust the Ordnance Survey.

(For instance, I live on Traeth Bach and am well aware that Afon Drwyryd flows either side of the great granite hump, Ynys Gifftin, that lies in the middle of the Traeth like some vast burial mound, dominating the waters all round. It IS an island, yet the present Ordnance Survey indicates it for the first time as a mere appendage to some very volatile saltings whose waters change every year.)

So Llyn Llymbrán it ought to be.

Since we are so dependent on the Ordnance Survey however, for directions, it must be Lliwbran in spite of our better judgement.

The intimations of the ancient king Bran from *The Mabinogion* are lost in this Ordnance Survey name, though of course it is impossible to tell if this association be the right one either. As Condry rightly points out, *bran* also means crow in Welsh, and it is astonishing that no lake seems to be named after the crow, particularly the *cigfran* (literally, meat-crow – or raven), a bird often sailing over lakes.

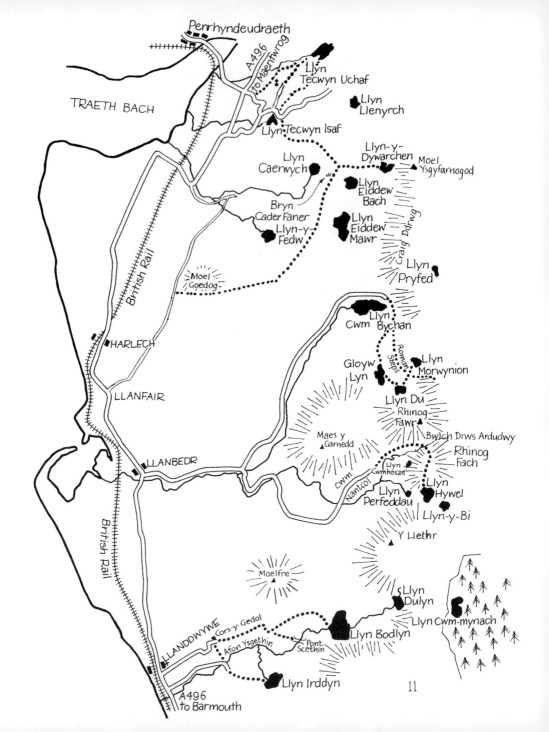

11

Eleven   Ardudwy

The cantref of Ardudwy is a secret place – not a hidden place, for that is practically an impossibility in a world where cars, coaches and even satellites in the stratosphere search out the remotest corners – but secret in the sense that it reserves to itself the vestiges of the deep past, of ancient peoples following their own ways and leaving behind deposits of inscrutable mystery. There is a sense of Ireland too, just over the shimmering sea below, which is rarely out of sight on this high and ancient western upland. Indeed, some of the primaeval piles of stones are named *cyttiau wyddelod* – Irishmen's huts.

Much of the heroic sagas of the *Mabinogion* is based in this area. It was from this area that the Welsh king Bendigeidfran sighted the Irishman Matholwch and his men in their longboats, with their shields held upside down in token of peace, a peace that was soon broken by Efnisien in his jealousy when his half-sister Branwen became espoused to Matholwch.

And there is a sense that here the drovers' roads, with their carefully wrought dry-stone walls climbing the glaciated humps and hollows, are part of that withdrawn past stretching back and removed from us by a whole gamut of circumstances like domestic and agrarian customs, religion, language and even physical appearance.

Yet drovers were still herding their cattle, pigs and geese over these hills until the railways took over the movement of livestock towards the end of the last century. So well defined are the drovers' roads and so well preserved the dry-stone walls that the three lakes of the Ysgethin valley are best reached by using these ancient ways.

602231 The base is the Gors-y-Gedol estate directly inland from the church of Llanddwywe on the Harlech–Barmouth road. From Gors-y-Gedol there is a choice of two ways, one turning south at right-angles through a gate and past a cromlech to the old bridge of Pont Fadog (and how beautiful it is with its dedication stone saying SAER 1762 – and inscrutable too since *saer* simply means a man who builds). The road then bears left and up into the valley
630220 towards the lowest of the three lakes, Llyn Irddyn.

But the best route for a full day out is to continue straight up from Gors-y-Gedol estate. Through the gate straight ahead the drovers' road begins at once, broad, with a paved centre and wide grass margins confined by dry-stone walls. The grass margins enabled the herds to graze as they went. The character of the walls is enhanced by the fact that most of the blocks are glacial boulders cleared from the land. What a monument to human effort they are, perhaps not as sad as the walls enclosing the little fields of Connemara in the west of Ireland but still with that memory of hard grinding work. They are also a monument to human canniness, for the walls did not only guide the flocks along, but kept them off the land on the other side. Land and pasture were wealth and once the herds were on the move, farmers were anxious to see that they did not spill over into their fields.

635235 The droves moved upwards towards Pont Scethin, between the middle lake Llyn Bodlyn, and Llyn Irddyn. On the way, two ruined *lletiau* or drovers' inns offered shelter for the night, with a corral for the beasts still well preserved. Pont Scethin itself is well worth pilgrimage, since it carried the old London Post road over the Ysgethin. But again it is perhaps best to pause before descending the slope to the bridge, at a cairn just before the conspicuous larch plantation which straggles up the slopes to Moelfre on the left. The drovers' way becomes a track, very wet
648240 in parts, and ends ultimately at Llyn Bodlyn at 1,248 feet above sea level.

Llyn Bodlyn is a reservoir and the water engineers have not been very sensitive with what must once have been a most beautiful lake under a protecting wall of vertical rock face some five hundred feet high. This wall is good climbing stuff, but sadly at the lakeside under the cliff stands a monument to William Haynes Ledbrook of Kenilworth, who fell and died there in 1913 at the age of twenty-one. With that name and with his taste for danger on the heights, he might have been a war poet and a most likely candidate for the subsequent holocaust of the Somme or Passchendaele.

Bodlyn is one of only four lakes where the *torgoch* lives, though as a layman I find it difficult to pin down the fishermen/naturalists as to the *torgoch*'s actual habitat. Furthermore this mystery is compounded by the legends from the past, for practically every visitor, like Pennant or Dr Johnson, has either made some original observation on this mysterious fish or has perpetuated some earlier legend, as often as not wrong. But perhaps that goes with fishermen. Anyway, Bodlyn seems to have been a fisherman's lake, hence the well-built boathouse. But there is no boat there at present. Bodlyn is a remote lake, inaccessible to all but the stoutest vehicles and far enough up the valley to deter the tripper. The curtain wall round the lake hardly enhances it, but still it is one of the most rewarding lakes in the whole area. As with many lakes, it is the context that counts, especially the wall of rock.

Llety on Drovers' Road: Ardudwy

Llyn Bodlyn

662244

A view towards the eastern ridge between Crib y Rhiw and Diffwys reveals a definite hollow five or six hundred feet higher up, unmistakably indicating a corrie lake and although the walk is quite strenuous after the long haul to Bodlyn, and involves boulders and bogland, it is well worth the extra effort. Llyn Dulyn with its singular rock islet is a gem. On the inner shore a few horsetails rise from the translucent under-water garden. At one spot a flat slab of exposed manganese shale invites the weary walker to stretch out for a while in the sun, if any. This manganese used to provide quite a bit of wealth in these parts and there were levels, now abandoned, dotted all over the place, mostly on the slopes above Barmouth.

The walk back to Gors-y-Gedol is long and hard, over rock and bog and once again down the drovers' road. But taken as a whole, this round of the two upper lakes is an excellent day's trip, with the added reward of a view of Llyn Irddyn over to the left, dazzling in the late afternoon light.

585268   Further north, branching inland off the Harlech–Barmouth road (A496) at Llanbedr, there is a narrow winding road through some of the finest natural woodland in North Wales. It leads ultimately to two wild upland valleys, Cwm Bychan straight ahead and Cwm Nantcol branching off to the right about one mile out from Llanbedr. The terrain is among the oldest rocks in the world, the Dome of Harlech, which is the core left after the erosion of the great dome that once humped over from Eryri to Cader Idris, now cut into a complex pattern of valleys by the Ice Age glaciers. Boulders strew the valley side of Cwm Bychan and it is interesting to see how the old dwarf oaks have settled their toes between them. A sparkling stream threads its way over the rocky floor and an occasional bridge, dating from pack-horse days, carries the ancient roads over it. Between the oaks on the valley floor the turf is the sweetest green in the country.

640313   Near the head of the valley, some four or five miles up, Llyn Cwm Bychan suddenly comes magnificently into view. At the far side, the slopes of Carreg-y-Saeth rise in heather terraces, and on to the ancient height of Rhinog Fawr. Glaciation is evident everywhere, with bed rock underfoot and worn striated boulders strewn all round. Cwm Bychan seems set apart from the world and the silence around the lake enhances this feeling. A buzzard soars overhead. Sheep graze the terraces, nibbling their way through heather to the succulent stuff underneath. And hereabouts, depending on luck and the weather, you catch a glimpse of one or two of the feral goats, mostly black and white, which have long been established in these wilder regions. They are magnificent, independent beasts, a nuisance to farmers but born survivors.

The road passes along the left side of the lake and ends at a farm. From there on the path leads, leaving the lake well behind, over the last meadows of the valley and up into the narrow defile called
653303   the Roman Steps, another drovers' path, to Bwlch Tyddiad, where there is a wonderful panorama to the east.

There are three hidden lakes in this area, captured in hollows on the slopes of Rhinog Fawr. It is very rough going over the heather and rock-strewn terraces, and though never severe, it is arduous
658303   walking. Llyn Morwynion (no relation, I imagine, to the same named lake near Ffestiniog which is associated with the story of

Llyn Cwm Bychan

646300

the Maidens of Ardudwy) lies on the left above the Steps, and Llyn Du with Gloyw Lyn to the right. I remember once walking up the Roman Steps and over the top of Rhinog Fawr and feeling so over-heated with the rough going on the way down that I stripped off at Gloyw Lyn (Bright Lake) and plunged in. I think it is the coldest swim I ever had, although it was midsummer and the sun hot in the heavens.

All this is terrain for only the most committed walkers. I have helped one man down Cwm Bychan. He was in agony with a sprained ankle. His boots were sound but brand new. He was far from sound and anything but new. You have to be fit and well equipped for country like Ardudwy. It seemed churlish to tell him he ought to stick to the lowland ways until he had lost a pound or two: he was quite white with pain and in no mood for advice.

600273　Back down the valley to the fork, the right branch crosses a bridge about a mile up from Llanbedr and carries another narrow valley road up to Cwm Nantcol, surely one of the best walks in North Wales. Sheer geological age abounds everywhere, with only the hardiest vegetation able to find sustenance. Higher up the cwm, the bilberry flourishes in great tufts. The Afon Cwm-Nantcol winds down, with an almost right-angle bend between Maes-y-Garnedd and Moelfre. Following this river to its source between the boulders and the bilberry is not very easy going, but

665282　it leads to one of the most dramatic cols in the area, Bwlch Drws Ardudwy (Pass of the Door of Ardudwy) and, of course, it was yet another of the several routes for the drovers out of the coastal stretch. Like the Roman Steps in neighbouring Cwm Bychan it offers a sweeping view to the east once the top is reached.

A stiff but not severe climb up the slopes of Rhinog Fach to the right offers superb views east and west, and though the initial climb is literally breathtaking, it is well worth the trouble, for the rolling top of Rhinog Fach is then pleasant going, unless a walker is foolish enough to risk windy weather or rain, when he might be blown away or bogged down. The descent on the south side reveals a lake hardly less spectacular than Llyn Dulyn: Llyn

664266　Hywel is not very large, it nestles under a col, with a great slab of smooth rock tilting into it on its upper side at an angle of 45 degrees, looking as fresh as though the glacier had melted but yesterday. Indeed the whole of this area has that look of having just emerged and warmed up after the Ice Age, with only the ingenious walls that thread along the slopes reminding us that man has been settled here since prehistoric times. Lower down a tributary valley falls again to Cwm Nantcol, beginning with a

659264　small lake that is gradually silting up, Llyn Perfeddau, a gruesome name meaning Lake of Entrails.

670264　Just over the other side of the col above Llyn Hywel on the east face lies another little cirque lake, Llyn-y-Bi (Magpie Lake). The whole walk over and around Rhinog Fach and its lakes is a long and exhausting day's work, not to be lightly undertaken, but extremely rewarding.

From the ridge walk over the top of Rhinog Fach, too, can be seen quite a number of lakes on the east side, besides Llyn-y-Bi. Six miles away to the north, the pale sheet of Llyn Trawsfynydd comes first; then a small innominate mere just over the way; beyond that another, like a small mirror, right under Craig Aberserw; and two miles away to the south-east, Llyn Cwm Mynach – just visible among the conifers of the highest plantation under Diffwys.

678237

The trail down from Llyn Hywel can take either the tributary falling out of Llyn Perfeddau or one closer in under the mountain via a small lake called Llyn Cwmhosan. The way down is covered with enormous block scree, so huge as to send the stream yards underground, whence it can be heard fighting its way among the blocks. The whole landscape is one great expanse of these blocks, either dragged away from their source by the glacier and dropped randomly or simply detached by ice from the exposed strata to fall away or even just tilt, in some cases like a pack of dominoes.

660277

Llyn Hywel and Rhinog Fach

A branch of the Gulf Stream runs up Cardigan Bay and warms the 'armpit' (*y gesail*, in Welsh; a much better rendering of the gentle, warm hollow of the arm) of Tremadog Bay between Harlech and Criccieth. This area is sheltered from the north by the mountains of Eryri and from the east by the heights of Ardudwy. The winters are mostly mild, with any snowfall along the coastline usually melted by midday.

In the upper extremity of this corner of the sea, a road from Penrhyndeudraeth crosses the toll-bridge over Afon Dwyryd as it enters Traeth Bach (the smaller of the two estuaries on either side of the Trwyn Penrhyn peninsula, the other being Traeth Mawr which Maddocks dammed at Porthmadog).

619385

This road crosses the main Harlech-Maentwrog road (A496) and almost at once climbs steeply up into the wilds of Ardudwy, but not before passing through an abundance of wild flowers in the lane-side and one of the richest lakes in North Wales, Llyn Tecwyn Isaf (lower). This lane bifurcates at Capel Bont Tecwyn. Take the left, signed as a cul-de-sac, and the lake is just over the brow, in its sheltered hollow surrounded by woods, but with a green sward along its shore-line.

629370

It is that sheltered aspect, and probably the base elements in the surrounding drainage area, that impart such richness and beauty on Llyn Tecwyn Isaf. All along its northern shore water-lilies, both yellow and white, flourish, punctuated by the thin spikes of water lobelia and the self-assertive trefoils of the bogbean.

There is much more – it is a botanist's paradise. There is even a eucalyptus hanging over the wall of the neighbouring estate to the west of the lake, where a peninsula springs out into the middle. Dab-chick and Little Grebe patter about in the far corner. It is a great pity that Llyn Tecwyn Isaf is accessible by car – how much more pleasurable it would be to arrive always on foot, having ascended that flower-rich lane with magnificent views over Cardigan Bay on the right.

The road by Llyn Tecwyn Isaf which branches off straight ahead leads up to Llandecwyn, an isolated church on its own eminence overlooking the bay and leading ultimately to the upper lake of the pair, Llyn Tecwyn Uchaf. A path further round at the head of Llyn Tecwyn Isaf, by the stream, is a more interesting way up to the wilder, humpy region of Llyn Tecwyn Uchaf, which is a reservoir, and though the lake is enhanced by the steep flanks on its northern shore, it has to be said that it is one of those lakes to which it is better to travel than to arrive, for the walk along the old pack-horse route through the native oak woods (very old too) is most diverting.

640382

The more direct route to the upper lake starts left at the bottom of the lane up to the lower lake. I find this the easier of the two routes: returning by the old path down to Llyn Tecwyn Isaf. That way there is the added reward of the views as you descend to the toll-bridge, with Harlech Castle in the distance silhouetted against the sea's horizon and Traeth Bach and Cardigan Bay laid out before you.

But a more strenuous day's walking on the steep heights above and south-west of Llyn Tecwyn Isaf will lead ultimately to another hollow below the flat summit of Mynydd Ysgyfarnogod. It is a very wild area not easily explored and can be extremely damp. There are no recognized paths.

647353

For the enthusiast, however, it can be immensely interesting, because in the midst of it, on a low rise on its own, is Bryn Cader Faner, a stone circle of great beauty, coronet shaped and most touching in its isolation. In prehistoric times it was on the path that led up from Llanfair by Moel Goedog, itself covered with hut circles and a cairn, and over to Trawsfynydd.

613324

654349

The lakes are of less consequence, either being silted up like Llyn-y-Dywarchen under the brow of Mynydd Ysgyfarnogod or very ordinary reservoirs like Llyn Eiddew Mawr below the steep crags of Craig Ddrwg (Bad Rock!). This is the largest of the group.

646337

646344 Llyn Eiddew Bach is just to its north, Llyn Caerwych further out
641350 to the north and Llyn-y-Fedw over west towards Moel Goedog.
625330 None of these lakes has the drama of the Ardudwy lakes further
south, like Llyn Hywel or Llyn Cwm Bychan.

But any lake is worth a visit, and I would advise only that the best
footwear is absolutely necessary for this stretch of country, plus a
good sense of terrain. There is a good alternative route to Bryn
Cader Faner as a centre for these upper lakes. It is the old
576296 pack-horse way which rises out of Llanfair (one and a half miles
south of Harlech on the A496). Three miles up, there is a fork, just
before Moel Goedog. Keep to the right of the hill and after a mile
Llyn-y-Fedw comes into view, then after another mile Llyn
Eiddew Mawr appears in a hollow on the right. Bryn Cader Faner
is a mile further on, its coronet shape in profile against the sky.

Llyn Tecwyn Isaf

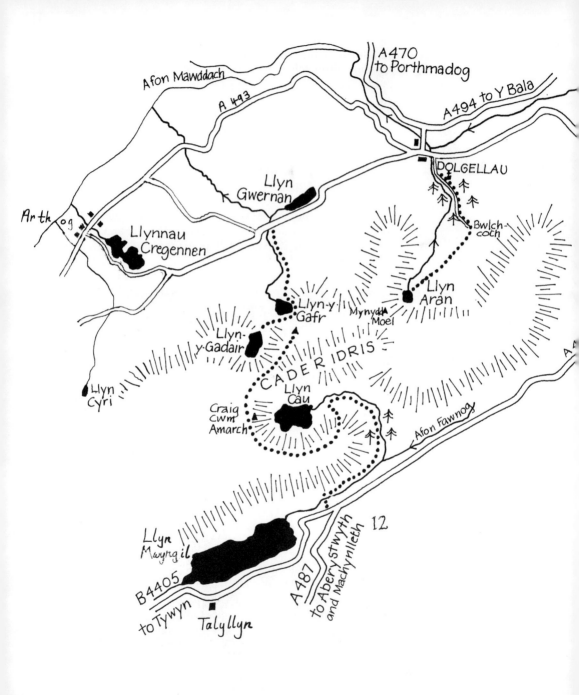

Twelve   Cader Idris

A 470 to
Dinas Mawddwy

730178 The great ridge that comprises Cader Idris and its outliers is
isolated from the rest of the highlands by two major divides: to
the north and west by the Mawddach estuary, and to the south
and east by the Bala-Talyllyn fault. The favourite centre for
exploring Cader is Dolgellau, of course, which like Betws-y-
Coed has a long tradition in comfortable hostelries for travellers.

From Dolgellau, the mountain appears to climb in massive steps,
but there is no recognized route *direttissimo* out of the town. Since
Cader Idris is a well-defined ridge with corries on both sides, it is
necessary for lake-walkers to explore either side, where the
corries hold well-celebrated cirque lakes.

766167 Starting from Dolgellau, the main road to Machynlleth (A487)
after the right turn at Cross Foxes travels down the Talyllyn
Fault. It is dramatic country, with fine views up the flanks of
Cader Idris on the right. The summit of Bwlch Talyllyn is
reached, the road winding through moraine, then falling in a long
spectacular run down the *bwlch*, with distant views of Llyn
Mwyngil or Lake Talyllyn.

732115 At the bottom, the road turns quite sharply left for Corris and
Machynlleth, with a spur to Tywyn leading straight ahead
towards the lake. Take this latter road, and after 150 yards there is
a path on the right, clearly defined as *the* ascent of Cader Idris, at
present still marked with a pair of old iron gates with the name
'Idris' on each.

There is also the mandatory '*Llwybr Cyhoeddus*' which always
marks a public path in Wales. On my last visit, this was pointing

in diametrically the opposite direction, *away* from the mountain! This is the starting-point of one of the greatest walks of all.

It is indeed *the* path up Cader. There are many others, for Cader, like Yr Wyddfa, is a mountain with several spurs, each offering an approach to the summit. But this path, if perhaps the most arduous, starting from less than 300 feet above sea level, is surely the most popular, for en route it offers an exceptional view of Llyn Cau.

The path soon crosses the Afon Fawnog and at once climbs the steep slopes through romantic woodland, following the tumbling torrent of Nant Cader. As the slope becomes less steep, the path gradually bears left, still more or less following the brook, until the great corrie begins to close in. Surely, this is the most spectacular corrie of all. Richard Wilson painted it in the mid-eighteenth century and it has attracted sightseers ever since. It is a long corrie, with an obvious rock barrier and moraine half-way up, holding back the lake. This rock barrier at one place emerges from the sheep-grass and morainic debris like a great smooth whale-back, a sort of immemorial Moby Dick, guardian of the cwm.

713124 All round this magnificent cwm, practically encircling it, the crags rise to the various pronounced peaks of Cader. Most spectacular of all is the clear pyramid of Craig Cwm-amarch (straight ahead). Once the rock barrier is cleared, the lake comes into view, lying under the great pointed crag with a classical perfection that must have appealed at once to Wilson, though it has to be said that he took rather too many liberties in order to adjust a classical composition to his satisfaction. His painting in the Walker Art Gallery in Liverpool, though among his best, hardly does justice to this amazing sight.

The crags rise blackly to the jagged sky-line, an almost perfect point to a vast pyramid, while below it, with its clearly defined shore-line, the lake is almost serene with a grateful grassy bank over its outflow, surely the proper viewpoint for perhaps the most magnificent lake of all. It is worthy of contemplation. Its sublimely deep cerulean colour provides the foil to the tumbled grass and boulders all round. This is nature's masterpiece.

But there is more, if there be time and energy. For a strenuous
ascent to the right of the head of the lake climbs to the shoulder
708125 between Craig Cwm-amarch and the summit itself, and this will
offer views downwards of Llyn Cau and also, incidentally, of the
other cirque lakes on the other side of the mountain, Llynnau
Gadair and Gafr. From that col, the summit is merely a twenty
minute slog to the right. And then, by returning to the col and
traversing the magnificent crags of Craig Cwm-amarch itself, the
views down to the lake are really sensational.

Those who suffer the least vertigo are recommended not to try it.
This is a view down one of the supreme examples of a long
glaciated cwm with its corries, first the steep initial erosion of the
crags, the blue-black lake at the bottom; then the bleached rocks
of the barrier and the morainic debris, and the long descent of the
lake's outflow, Nant Cader.

The ascent from the road to the lake is a decent afternoon's work,
but the long traverse requires a full day if justice is to be done.

After Llyn Cau, anything else would seem an anticlimax. But
even so, there is a quite gentle walk up to the corrie lakes on the
northern face of Cader. Travelling west out of Dolgellau on the
main Tywyn road (A493), there is a fork left just after the church
which carries on up a fair gradient. A few miles along it returns
ultimately to the main Dolgellau–Tywyn road via Llynnau
698152 Cregennen (about which later) at Arthog. But the parking place
for the ascent to the northern cirque lakes of Cader is near Ty'n
Ceunant about 3 miles from Dolgellau.

The path progresses steadily from there on, and after the drama of
710141 Llyn Cau it is expecting too much of Llyn Gafr which comes first
708136 en route, or Llyn-y-Gadair, to match it. But in fact, once the latter
is reached, at 1,837 feet, the view of the lake in its corrie is
impressive.

It lies more directly under the summit than Llyn Cau, whose
dominating cliff is Craig Cwm-amarch. Perhaps it is that clarity
of outline and its relation with the cliff-face which give Llyn Cau
the edge over its neighbours, and indeed, over any in North
Wales.

Craig Cwm-Amarch

735139 There is one further little corrie lake under Cader Idris, on the north side of its eastern extremity. It is Llyn Aran. However small, it shares with all the corrie lakes on Cader Idris the distinction of having a fine cliff behind it, Mynydd Moel, at 2,804 feet, not far below the summit. Its stream is the same that flows so charmingly through Dolgellau itself. Since the lake is at nearly 1,600 feet above sea level and 3 miles from the town, it is quite a strenuous walk, not to be lightly undertaken. Start and keep on the east side of the stream and after reaching Bwlch-coch keep the stream on the right.

660145 By contrast, Llynnau Cregennen take no great effort to reach and are a popular walk from Dolgellau along the Ty'n Ceunant road which, incidentally, passes Llyn Gwernan at the roadside, about two and a half miles out of Dolgellau. Llynnau Cregennen are really Arthog's lakes, however much the larger market town claims them on its list of recommended walks in its guide book.

Not everyone who stays at the popular resort of Arthog, at the mouth of the Mawddach estuary, realizes that the little river that flows through it has its source in a corrie on Cader Idris. But if followed up (there is no recognized path), it lies under the westernmost knob of the ridge of Cader, Braich Ddu. It is tiny
658118 Llyn Cyri, at a height of 1,150 feet above sea level.

The entire long south-east flank of Cader Idris falls away so steeply and dramatically as to indicate to the most unprofessional eyes more than glaciation. It is one side of the Bala-Talyllyn Fault – the largest land shift in Wales. Not only did the valley fall away, but the southern, relative to the northern, side has moved some two miles adrift, inland.

It is no wonder then that two of Wales's most beautiful sheets of water should be found in this Fault and should have celebratory names: Llyn Tegid ('Beautiful Lake') and Llyn Mwyngil ('Lake in the Pleasant Retreat').

Descending from Craig Cwm-amarch along the outer rim above Llyn Cau, the fault is most apparent. It is a long (very long) steep
720100 slope down to the floor of the valley. And there lies Llyn Mwyngil (or Talyllyn Lake, as it is known, after the little settlement round the hotels at its foot).

It is a roadside lake, therefore easily accessible on the route that follows the floor of the valley from Cross Foxes to Tywyn (B4405). Despite this accessibility, Llyn Mwyngil still has the air of pleasant retreat that gives it its name. A handsome old anglers' inn on its shore provides a welcome for those privileged to fish in the lake and seems, in its outward aspect, to be little changed since the nineteenth century.

Llyn Mwyngil is a lake rich in its fish and its flora. Its yellow water-lily is rather special, being the hybrid between the common yellow and the least yellow water-lilies, though neither of its parents exists in the lake. It is a shallow lake. The stream that falls from Cwm-amarch is building quite a delta and presages eventual silting.

Lying in its deep rift valley under Cader's greenest slope, Llyn Mwyngil is best visited off-season. It is a place to enjoy, not for sunshine, nor for the more usual holiday reasons, but for its sweet peace. May and October are lovely on and round it. Winter is marvellous at Talyllyn, for even when there is a freeze-up, there are still areas where duck and swans create water patterns as they feed.

Appendix

T. J. Jehu: (1902). Bathymetrical Survey of the Lakes of Snowdonia. *Transactions of the Royal Society of Edinburgh 40: 25–40.*

T. J. Jehu's paper outlines first the paucity of information on the Welsh Lakes compared with the English Lakes and the Swiss ones.

The first significant difference is that while in some of the English lakes, the bottom lies below sea level, in the Welsh lakes in no case does this occur. In general most Welsh lakes are situated higher than the English lakes.

Jehu's soundings confirmed his thesis that most Welsh lakes lay in rock basins, although some are partly rock basins and partly barrier basins, and a few simply barrier basins.

Jehu was not the first on the scene. Sir Andrew Ramsey in his memoir on *The Geology of North Wales* (1881) had stated that the Revd. W. T. Kingsley had been sounding the lakes of North Wales with a view to proving them to be true rock-bound basins. But his findings were not published. Ramsey was associated with glacial surveys in Switzerland and North Wales.

W. W. Watts published 'Notes on some tarns near Snowdon' in the *Geological Magazine*, 1895. Mr Brend in the same magazine in 1897 published researches on the East Caernarvonshire lakes and was almost certain that Llyn Crafnant lay in a rock basin.

Jehu's thesis, however, seemed to establish once and for all the glacial origin of the lakes of Snowdonia. He published tables on only 15 major lakes, though these encompassed a large range of differences in both altitude and depth as can be seen from the tables below.

Lake	Elevation above sea level	Max. depth	Mean depth
Gwynant	215	54	18.6
Dinas	175	30	12.9
Idwal	1,223	36	11
Crafnant	602	71	31
Padarn	339	94	52.4
Peris	339	114	63.9
Llydaw	1,416	190	77.4
Glaslyn	1,970	127	62.6
Cwellyn	463	122	74.1
Ogwen	984	10	6.8
Cowlyd	1,164	222	109.1
Mymbyr	588	29	10
Eigiau	1,219	32	9.2
Geirionydd	616	48	21.3
Dulyn	1,747	189	104.2

Bibliography

It is some years since I gave up my small printing and publishing concern The Cidron Press, as a distraction from my principal activities as walker and artist. One of its publications, E. G. Rowland's *Hill-walking in Snowdonia*, has passed through several hands since I gave it away to an indigent climber/student, is still in print somewhere or other, and remains in my opinion the best walking guide to the mountains of Snowdonia. 'Rowlie' was a Civil Servant, looking after Weights and Measures, and if his duties required him at a grocer's shop in Beddgelert say, he would walk straight over the top from his home in Criccieth, taking in the summit of Moel Hebog on the way. So he totted up more peaks per annum than any man I know. His little book remains a classic, and I miss my association with Rowlie as climber and writer. While he has been exploring the Elysian fields for a year or two now, I have carried on his tradition of making work fit pleasure, or the other way round. Thus I find I have totted up lakes much as he totted up peaks. His book *The Ascent of Snowdon* – written, I remember, in pique over John Hunt's *The Ascent of Everest* – is the best walking companion to Yr Wyddfa itself, but it too is out of print since I gave up printing and publishing.

The New Naturalist *The Snowdonia National Park* by William Condry (Collins, 1966) is the best and most comprehensive guide to the area as a whole, covering its natural history, geology and topography. The older New Naturalist *Snowdonia* by North, Campbell and Scott (1949) was in some ways more interesting, offering a better historic view, including industrial history, and devoting a special section to the lakes. Both these volumes bear excellent bibliographies for those wishing to extend their study of the area.

My own favourite volume remains, however, *The Mountains of Snowdonia* by Carr and Lister, 'Members of the Alpine Club' 1924, reissued in 1948 and now, alas, out of print. It may be out of date in some respects but it is still among the best reading on the natural history of the region, including the lakes, and is particularly attentive to the eccentric needs of anglers.

The Shell Guide *North Wales* by Beazley and Brett (Faber, 1971) offers an assessment of the lakes, and like book reviews, it is interesting to compare personal experience with theirs. Brett's photograph of Llyn Peris is a sad reminder of lost beauty.

Challinor and Bates on *Geology explained in North Wales* (David & Charles, 1973) is not exactly for the layman, despite its title, but it is a useful guide to the region's structure.

There are many travellers' books on North Wales, dating from Giraldus Cambrensis (1188) *Itinerary*, which takes in some of our lakes, including first mention of Llyn-y-Dywarchen's floating island.

Humphrey Llwyd (1584) *A Description of Cambria*, Thomas Pennant (1784) *A Tour in Wales*, and, of course, that old gossip George Borrow (1862) *Wild Wales* are a fair guide through the ages.

Entertaining, if not terribly informative is A. G. Bradley's (1898) *Highways and Byways in North Wales*, though it is more highways than byways, so he missed more than he saw, especially lakes.

The Lakes of Wales – A Guide for Anglers and Others (Herbert Jenkins, 1931) by Frank Ward is certainly an impressive list, and some of the photographs (Llyn Elsi uncluttered by Forestry) demonstrate the change in environment in a mere generation.

The rare and beautiful *A Prospect of Wales* (King Penguin, 1948) by Gwyn Jones is most desirable but practically unobtainable, in fact a collector's item.

The best translation of *The Mabinogion* (Everyman's Library, 1949) is by Gwyn Jones and Thomas Jones.

Lastly, Shirley Toulson's *The Drovers' Roads of Wales* (Wildwood House, 1977) is an invaluable guide on the old hill routes, such as Cwmorthin or Cwm Croesor, used by the drovers and their livestock. Since water was a first requisite, lakes often figured in their navigations.

Index